Beyond Progressive Education

Titles in the Crisis Points series

Beyond Progressive Education

Ken Jones

M

First published 1983 by
THE MACMILLAN PRESS LTD
London and Basingstoke
Companies and representatives throughout the world

ISBN 0 333 30739 9 (hard cover)
ISBN 0 333 30740 2 (paper cover)

Typeset in Great Britain by
WESSEX TYPESETTERS LTD
Frome, Somerset

Printed and bound in Great Britain
at The Pitman Press, Bath

Contents

Acknowledgements

I would like to thank all those with whom I have discussed the ideas developed in this book – particularly Richard Hatcher, Will Reese and Bernard Regan. I would like to thank Phil Cohen and Clara Mulhern for reading and commenting upon the manuscript, and Steven Kennedy for his patient and constructive editorial advice.

I am particularly grateful to Hilda Kean, whose supply of information has been inexhaustible, and whose criticisms were helpfully challenging. Her dissertation, referred to in the endnotes, is an extremely valuable source of information on the socialist educational movements of the first three decades of the century. It has been well plundered in the preparation of this text.

December 1982   KEN JONES

Abbreviations

ACE	(Labour Party) Advisory Committee on Education
AMMA	Assistant Masters and Mistresses Association
APU	Assessment of Performance Unit
CBI	Confederation of British Industry
CP	Communist Party (of Great Britain)
CSE	Certificate of Secondary Education
DES	Department of Education and Science
EPA	Educational Priority Area
EWI	Educational Workers' International
ILEA	Inner London Education Authority
ILP	Independent Labour Party
IMF	International Monetary Fund
LEA	Local Education Authority
MAT	Mixed Ability Teaching
MSC	Manpower Services Commission
NAHT	National Association of Head Teachers
NALT	National Association of Labour Teachers
NAS	National Association of Schoolmasters *later to become*
NAS/UWT	National Association of Schoolmasters/Union of Women Teachers
NUSS	National Union of School Students
NUT	National Union of Teachers
NUWT	National Union of Women Teachers
OECD	Organisation for Economic Co-operation and Development
PAT	Professional Association of Teachers

SHA	Secondary Heads' Association
STA	Socialist Teachers' Alliance
SWP	Socialist Workers' Party
TES	(The) Times Educational Supplement
TLK	Teaching London Kids
TLL	Teachers' Labour League
TUC	Trades Union Congress
YOP	Youth Opportunities Programme

A Note on Terms Used

The scope of this book is limited to the English school system. 'English' means just that: Scotland, Wales and the north of Ireland are scarcely touched upon. In general, the book does not deal with higher, further or adult education. When 'education' is used it is in a sense which most often excludes these sectors.

I have used the term 'labour movement' to refer to the trade unions and the Labour Party together. I do not intend it to carry a sentimental or uncritical significance – cf. 'this great movement of ours'.

When I refer on occasions to 'the Left', I intend to mean those socialist organisations and individuals who stand outside the mainstream traditions of reform. The term is a convenient shorthand; its use is not intended to imply that all who lie outside its scope form a monolithic and right-wing bloc.

Lastly, I have retained, without further comment than this, the original use in quoted material of 'he' and 'his' as pronouns which indicate a common gender.

K.J.

Introduction

Two orthodoxies

This book is about the two 'strategies' for educational reform which have dominated most of the last fifty years of English schooling. It deals with their evolution, consolidation and present decline.

The two strategies – those of 'equal opportunity' and of 'progressive education' – are interrelated. The first of them – the persistent movement to equalise educational opportunity – originated in the trade unions and in the Labour Party. Later it received support from many outside these organisations and for a time became the official ideology of state education. It has twice, in 1944 and again in the 1960s, inspired a reorganising of the structures of state education. It has been complemented by a second type of reform, centred on the changes in the curriculum and the regime of the school, demanded from the standpoint of progressive education. This approach, too, developing from the fringes of the education system, eventually achieved official endorsement, and was promulgated by institutions of teacher education and the leading agencies of curricular reform.

Neither 'equal opportunity' nor 'progressive education' is reducible to a coherent and plainly articulated programme. Each comprises several trends, with divergent emphases. Equal opportunity, for instance, has meant for some a more efficient means of producing 'qualified young people'.[1] For others, a minority, it has entailed an attack on educational institutions seen to be bastions of privilege. One argument stresses the economic rewards of equalising opportunity; the impulse of the other is egalitarian. Yet the positions have rarely been counterposed, and have frequently intermingled.

Progressive education is yet more of a mixture. It touches on issues of discipline, curriculum content and pedagogy; it is understood to be critical of authoritarianism, committed to the development of the 'whole person' and attentive to a psychology of learning. It, too, has variously been presented as the educational salvation of the working class and as the most efficient means of reproducing through the school the qualities required by a developed capitalism. But no progressive manifesto exists that tries to codify its aims.

The ease with which these approaches modulate their emphases and switch their *raisons d'être* is one of their most striking features. If the term 'strategy' is understood to combine the conscious formulation of objectives, the development of a coherent ideology to accompany them, and the construction of a committed social basis of support, then it must be used with caution and qualification. Around the issue, in particular, of whose interests the reforms promoted by 'equal opportunity' and 'progressive education' are intended to serve, there exists a fundamental vagueness, and this has affected the formulation of policy and the development of support. Such an incoherence has assisted the absorption of what have occasionally been radical critiques of state schooling into projects for the modernisation of the school in which the technocratic element has taken precedence over the egalitarian.

These 'strategies' became, especially in the 1960s and early 1970s, an orthodoxy which guided curriculum changes and defined educational purpose. Their influence within the education sector was considerable, yet was not matched by a comparable degree of popular understanding. As a result both of the equivocation at the heart of their ideas and of their narrow social base, they have been recently vulnerable to attacks originating both from new turns in state education policy under Labour, and from an educational Thatcherism.

The aims of this book are to account for the weaknesses of 'equal opportunity' and of 'progressive education', to explain the success that a right-wing counter-offensive has gained, and to discuss the outlines of an alternative Left strategy. Such a project takes it on to historical ground, for in atempting to found a new politics of education it is essential to describe, analyse, and criticise the old. Attempts to reorganise educational perspectives – such as the Black Papers and the Great Debate – have made such an attempt, and those concerned to develop a socialist educational politics can learn much from the success of their methods.

Thus the book begins with an attempt to evaluate the political objectives and the related ideologies of the main reforming traditions. It is in this context that its title should be understood. Why '*Beyond*' *Progressive Education*? After all, we have not arrived at a truly progressive stage of education, and one could argue that to announce the need to surpass it is both utopian and mischevious, since it distracts from the main task of reform.

But the case I try to make does not rest upon the dismissal of the fight for reform, nor of the struggle to implement some of the basic methods and working assumptions of progressive teaching. Rather, it distinguishes between these individual reforms and the general framework of ideology and politics in which they are set – a framework which has provided the language in which post-war educational objectives have, until recently, been discussed. Throughout this period governments, and employers too, have spoken the language of expanded opportunity and curriculum change. Today, since its vocabulary does not provide the terms in which pressing problems of technical and social need can be spoken, they are rejecting it for a more timely tongue. This book argues that if the supporters of reform continue to speak the old language, they will find themselves incapable both of discussing new problems in a radical way, and of winning popular support.

Four common elements

In Chapters 1 and 2 I look more closely at these related strategies. Here, it is enough to make four points. First, that at their common core is the conviction that the reforms they promote can both enhance the lives of individual students and at the same time serve the needs of nation and industry more effectively. Second, that they have together cultivated and rested on a substantial consensus among the different classes about educational objectives. Relatedly (since consensus makes necessary no sharper instruments) they have on nearly all occasions adopted the tactics of a pressure group, rather than of a campaigning movement, and have seen state initiative as the motor of change. In this way, they have gained influence at every level of educational organisation. Third, they have accepted that education is an activity that is, in ideological terms, neutral, or capable of being rendered so. Correspondingly, the teacher is seen as a humane and trusted professional, rather than as an authoritarian or any sort of political partisan. Last, it is necessary to make a point of qualification: these are both 'official' ideologies. They have affected policy-making and their influence has been widely diffused through the school system. But they do not represent the situation 'on the ground'. The daily workings of the school system necessarily produce forms of discrimination and discipline that are often remote from the intentions of reform. (Some of the discrepancies are referred to in Chapter 1.)

Reform challenged

This ensemble of beliefs is now under stress. The interest of present educational debate lies in the fact that, for the first time since 1930, ideologies and politics of reform are on the defensive, and different objectives have taken over the centre of debate; the 'crisis in education' is in large part a crisis of the traditional strategies of reform.

The connection between 'education for individual growth' and national need has become problematic. From 1975 onwards, with the onset of recession, the statements of government and industry have made it plain that the two aims contradict each other. New strategies have challenged those of reform. 'School and work' – the relation of education to vocational training, and to ideological preparation for work – has replaced equal opportunity as the central motif of state strategy. New kinds of state initiative have been taken – most notably the Manpower Services Commission and the New Training Initiative. Previous major changes, such as comprehensive reorganisation, had been related, at least in part, to the achievement of equal opportunity. In the 1970s, however, the major growth area – 16–19 education and training – was inspired more by fear of youth unemployment and industrial incapacity than by concern for opportunity.

But the changes in educational debate and policy were not only the result of state initiative. The revival of right-wing ideologies had an important effect in undermining educational consensus. The Black Papers and the Conservative polemics that followed them have a sense of urgency and crisis more acute than anything in the reforming tradition. The right has been able to use, compellingly, a language of purposefulness. 'Standards', 'excellence', 'order': these terms resound with an awareness that all is not well with education, and with a crusading determination to change it. That the Conservative Party, in its 1979 election campaign, felt able to utilise as a major slogan 'Educashun isn't working', is some measure of the initiative gained by the right. It is difficult to discover a similar verve in the language of reform.

Thus, as I try to show in Chapter 3, the high ground of educational debate – that which defines long-term strategy and purpose – is more and more occupied by interests radically different from those that have dominated the last half-century. Whereas progressive education now reacts defensively, the definition of problems, the marking out of the terrain of debate, are the work either of supporters of the 'school and work' connection or of the political right. Although reform still holds strong sectoral pockets of resistance – among teachers, lecturers, administrators – within the education system, it no longer determines the general outline of policy and debate, and has not proved capable of a popular response to the criticisms of the right.

Some forms of this crisis in strategy are obvious enough. Education cuts, the official discouragement of mixed ability teaching,[2] Conservative limitations on the growth of comprehensives – it would be comfortable to see these as the predictable and passing responses of 'reaction to equality'. But the problems are not all of this kind, external to the traditions of reform. It is not the case that the commitment to reform endures, despite a momentary containment. It is rather that its strategies face internal crisis and cannot respond to the effects of mass unemployment, social disaffection and intensified industrial demand upon them.

The result is not the utter obliteration of 'equal opportunity' as a motivating slogan. It is quite capable of sustaining defensive struggles against the most obnoxious features of Conservative policy, and of generating educational initiatives that can find a subsidiary place in an overall policy whose inspiration is more utilitarian. In the wake of Brixton and Toxteth, for instance, multi-cultural education will become a positive boom-town of curriculum development. And, as the connection between school and work is developed, so many of the techniques associated with progressive education – self-directed learning, the search for student motivation – will be exploited. But these are activities that can no longer rest on a confidently founded educational *raison d'être*, supported by state policy and related to a particular social purpose; they are activities that are not defended by an elaborated philosophy, that fit into no coherent framework of general practice, and that are liable to appropriation by other strategies. Even the most complete attempts to redevelop an educational programme – those of the Labour Party[3] – combine opposition to privilege and the desire to widen access to higher education with an acceptance of ideas about school and work that do not break free from a 'needs of industry' model. Such an acceptance, in the context of a chronic British economic crisis, will do nothing to transform the content of mass education.

Socialist alternatives

This book, in Chapters 3 and 4, attempts to treat these weaknesses in some detail. It also, in Chapter 5, considers some of the attempts that have been made, from the 1920s onwards, to develop educational perspectives independent of those connected with equal opportunity, and concerned not only to increase access to education, but also to attempt to establish in the school a curriculum critical of, rather than subordinate to, the dominant demands made of education. It is those groups, currents, and movements that have, in the name of socialist objectives, made such an attempt, that I describe as 'the left', in the sense that they stand to that side of traditional Labour Party and trade-union strategies. But it cannot be said that their various activities have yet produced a convincing intellectual or political alternative to those strategies. It is true that there is, now, a multiplicity of radical practices: an infiltration of the classroom by previously forbidden topics of race, sex and class; a rejection of those explanations of working-class 'failure' that locate the problem in the inherent inadequacies of the working-class community; an alertness to some of the ways – literary, filmic, pictorial – in which ideology is reproduced; a scepticism about the plausibility of 'equal opportunity' as an attainable goal within the present social system; an opposition to ideologies of professionalism in the teacher trade unions. But these practices are fragmented, as well as legion. They are pursued in individual classrooms, with no sustaining organisation beyond a slender network of magazines and occasional conferences – or else are partially reflected in work within the NUT that cannot help but be affected by the demands and routines of trade unionism. They do not add up to a convincing alternative to reforming traditions. The left's general goals remain those formulated within the tradition of reform, and its political framework has added nothing more than trade-union militancy and classroom activism to the strategies and alliances worked out elsewhere. In particular, the left has now little systematic and collective to say about the content of schooling – what should be learnt, what education is appropriate to socialist ends – and about control: how can working-class and popular influence be exerted on those institutions that have normally been both state-administered and thought to exist above the realm of politics?

Content and control: these issues are, for a reforming outlook, of minor interest. But they would be of much greater importance in a socialist response to the present crisis, since they allow concern with questions of educational purpose and with the involvement of working-class and popular organisations in defining that purpose: issues crucial to the recapturing of ground from the right and centre.

It is here that the forgotten aspects of socialist education become valuable. The important works of Brian Simon and Harold Entwistle have made a rather one-sided contribution to identifying a socialist educational tradition. Simon, although he details some of the activity of the movements for independent working-class education, is not much concerned with radical movements in the state sector.[4] The effect is to present perspectives for state reform as the limit of socialist strategy. Entwistle also,[5] in claiming Antonio Gramsci as an educational conservative, concerned more with questions of access to a high level of general education, than with ideology, wrongly asserts that such a view 'exactly parallels that of the traditional European left'.

Neglect of this sort does the militant past a disservice, and in the present disarms us. The 'traditional' attitude of the important left wing of the labour movement in France and Germany between 1917 and 1933 consisted of a critical attitude to the knowledge conveyed by the school, and of an utter hostility to its fundamental purposes, combined with insistence on its authoritarian and primitive character. On the other hand, it was concerned with the different content and educational method involved in socialist education, as well as with the different relationship that it involved between the school and social and productive life. The self-organisation of students, the political integration of teachers with the working-class movement, the transformation of education into a means of understanding politics and production – these, more than access, were its characteristic themes. They contrast not only with those of reform but with the radical practice of the recent past.

One of the criticisms that will be made of the educational radicalism of the 1960s and 1970s is informed by this alternative tradition: that it was a radicalism that did not concern itself so much with programmes of educational change, as with taking practical advantage of the openings created by official support for reform and for progressive education. While this no doubt avoided scholastic debate and allowed innovation to thrive, it inhibited responses to the change in ideological climate that occurred after 1975. There existed no clear definition of educational purpose against which proposals for 'education for industry' could be assessed. Similarly, the insistence of earlier socialists on establishing direct popular control of education would have at least established some basis for popular scrutiny of the system, and some dialogue between teachers' and trade-union and other organisations. As it was, the sectoral introversion of teachers of all political descriptions gave an advantage to the right, which was well able to raise the slogan of accountability against any murmur of radicalism.

I argue, in Chapters 5 and 6, that to answer, from a socialist viewpoint, questions raised in the present educational debate entails breaking from one tradition to rediscover another: going beyond requires looking back. I look back, in particular, to the discussions of Marxist or Marxist-influenced organisations –

especially those of the Teachers' Labour League in the 1920s, and also, though to a much lesser extent, the various movements that re-established educational radicalism in the late 1960s. I find here both an interest in educational strategy – an attempt to find social forces that can support and develop particular ideas – and, though less frequently, an attempt to develop educational ideas which have not tacitly assumed a relationship between school and work of a functional kind. But the book is not written in an archaeo-Marxist zeal to revive an unblemished tradition. The encounters of Marxist organisations with 'equal opportunity' and progressive education have too often been brief and unsatisfactory. Too often, Marxists have made an arch-priority of their day-to-day work in the educational unions. When they have turned aside to educational issues, their criticisms have tended to be rough and superficial, based on an analysis of the political 'line' of the progressives, at the expense of examining the specifically educational content of their work. On the other hand, perhaps more typically, they have taken on board not just a defence of particular reforms, but an endorsement of the educational–political outlook of the reforming currents. To earn the credentials for a role as critic and strategist, Marxists have to judge their own heritage most soberly.

It would also be foolish to pretend that a Marxist contribution to current strategy can be derived from a simple reiteration of past strengths. Compared with the 1920s, its political zenith, Marxism today faces more complex problems. Whereas it then confronted a school system resting very clearly on force and extremes of inequality, it now faces a system relying on different means of inculcating consent and capable of offering a wider education to all and a degree of social mobility to some. On the other hand, Marxists address a working class far less accustomed to radical definition of its social and political goals, and not self-evidently enthusiastic for sweeping educational reform. In addition, they must comprehend new issues – a 'youth revolt', a consciousness of women's oppression – which they are far from fully appreciating.

For Marxism to make its concerns a live issue is thus a difficult task. Nevertheless, the political conditions in which this work has to be done are not entirely unfavourable. Although the educational radicalism of working-class organisations is weaker than in the past, that of teachers, though very uneven, is much stronger. There are limited but still significant reserves of classroom and teacher trade-union activity that can be drawn upon. The shaking of its traditional ideologies has left some parts of the labour movement open to debate about changes in its educational policy. Other popular movements, in particular the women's movement, have challenged the existing system in the name of principles more radical than that of a simple increase in provision. They have been concerned to show how the school both presents a distorted knowledge and operates in a way whose daily functioning prevents the full participation of, for example, girl students.

Here at least are some grounds in which a new educational politics can take root. If it is to grow, it has to concern itself not only with the 'bread and butter' of classroom and trade-union work but with the richer and more complex issues of educational purpose, of alliance between teachers and non-teachers, of the ways in which the influence of such an alliance can be exerted upon the system. A tentative effort to develop some of these themes is made in the final chapter. It will have been worthwhile if others sufficiently value these suggestions to criticise and develop them.

1

The limits of reform

Two interpretations

In the eyes of the (Labour) politicians who have most seriously
pursued it, educational reform has had two aspects: the equalising
of opportunity and the weakening of 'class privilege' in the
education system. These goals have not been seen to depend upon a
socialist transformation of society, but have most often been
pursued as part of an attempt to modernise education, in response
to national economic need. Thus, Antony Crosland, Secretary of
State in the mid-1960s, advocated the ending of the public-school
system and promoted wide-scale comprehensive reorganisation.
Similarly, in the 1980s, Neil Kinnock has called for education to be
a 'finger in the fist of progress' represented by the industrial policy
of a future Labour Government, and has argued for the extension
of the comprehensive principle to post-16 education and, again, for
measures that would severely curtail public-school education. Each
of these views identifies a 'class bias' in the English schools which
prevents modernisation, promotes injustice and hinders industrial
adaptability. However, it is plain that Crosland was not successful
in eradicating or mitigating this bias, and it is not at all clear that
Kinnock's line of march is leading to a happier destination.
Reformers of the school have tended to underestimate the
intractability of the problem. To equalise opportunity entails
opposition to the basic constraints that the economic system applies
to education. Some are directly financial – cash restrictions, short-
and long-term, on public education. Others arise from the social

division of labour and its associated hierarchies of knowledge and control, so that there are tendencies to exclude the majority of students from knowledge beyond that which arises from the immediate requirements of labour and citizenship. These tendencies are embedded in the daily routines of schooling – in its exams, patterns of selection, course content and discipline, as well as in the attitudes of teachers and students.

Reform of the school cannot in itself, of course, affect the structures of society and economy outside. But it is not impossible to encourage an education that resists the continual pressure to prepare students for menial political and economic roles, and that, in the process, can stimulate a criticism of the system that makes such demands. More clearly, opportunities have arisen where an attack on particular kinds of segregation and privilege have been quite possible: an attack, for instance, on private education.

However, the record of educational reformers – and in this chapter I refer mainly to those associated with the labour movement – has in neither area been impressive. The relation between education and the economy has not been a matter for critical concern, and commitment to reforms of the second type has been half-hearted. This double failure has had two consequences. First, the reforming tradition has been unable to relate to and criticise the experience that the majority of the working population have had of the school – the stunted kind of knowledge it offers, its demotivating stress on discipline and control. Second, it has left educational reaction in possession of a number of bases, which are defended, like the grammar school, with greater and greater confidence and intensity, and from which its influence can be extended. The activities of the Thatcher government go to prove this latter contention: not only are existing grammar schools preserved, but they are allowed to extend their catchment areas into neighbouring LEAs which had previously been all-comprehensive.

The account that follows deals with the limits imposed upon reformers by their inability to respond to these problems. But it also considers the other side of the coin: the obstacles placed by the ideas of reformers in the way of an adequately close relationship between education and the 'objective' needs of a capitalist economy. That a set of policies expresses no hostility to the basic principles of an economic order is no guarantee that it will always effectively serve that order.

Education for all?

Equal opportunity promised greater access to education for all classes, and in particular for the working class. The result of such access would be that occupational destiny would no longer depend upon original social class. Equal opportunity thus set itself up in opposition to some of the basic inegalitarian tendencies in society – even though it aimed, in this respect, at no more than the placing of different personnel in the slots of a division of labour that itself remained unchanged. It has been frequently shown that this project has had only a very limited success. 'There is no sign that mobility could rise on a scale to produce anything like the state of equal opportunity to which conventional ideology and policy claim to aspire.' Even the expansion of opportunity that has occurred 'has involved an expansion of opportunity for the children of wealthy and ''middle-class' homes as well as for children of the common people: in some ways more for the former than the latter'. For example, 'the growth of student places in higher education from the early sixties met a demand which, in effect, came mainly from professional, managerial and other non-manual homes'.[1]

In the same way, several decades of equal opportunity have brought relatively little benefit to women, or, more recently, to black students. Far more boys than girls go on to take degree courses and 'any [post-school] education is generically more common for men than for women'.[2] For black students, the prospect of higher education is more remote, and the chances of getting any job are lower than those of whites.[3]

It is thus difficult to maintain that the promotion of equal opportunity has had the effects often claimed for it. Nevertheless, it could still be argued that even if educational outcome hasn't been substantially affected, then at least the quality of education available to working-class students is higher now than at any previous time. In some senses, this is true: the school-leaving age has, since 1944, twice been raised; more students go into higher education; more pass public exams; the curriculum is broader than that of the old elementary school, and the school regime is milder and more conducive to learning. But these advances are only very relative. The main feature of English education is still its provision of mass low-level schooling, with a continued emphasis on basic skills and control. The Inspectorate's survey of primary schools in

1978 unwittingly measured the rudimentary nature of much pre-secondary education: it is, still, elementary. The inspectors noted that 'teachers work hard to make pupils well-behaved, literate and numerate'. But, beyond that, they found many reasons for criticism. The 'basic skills' were well taught, but

> more could be done . . . to encourage them to follow a line of argument, to evaluate evidence, to reach judgements . . . Much of the writing done in the name of topic work amounts to no more than copying . . . It was rare to find children presented with a writing task which involved presenting a coherent argument . . . In about one third of the classes . . . children were spending too much time undertaking somewhat repetitive practice of processes which they had already mastered.

The curriculum was very narrow. 'Few primary schools . . . had effective programmes for the teaching of science . . . It was rare to find classes where the work was leading the children towards an understanding of historical change.'[4] These failings were not said to be the result of misguided progressive efforts; the inspectors found that three-quarters of the classes they surveyed were taught with a 'mainly didactic approach'.

In these several respects, then, the primary school is still a 'school for the masses'. It is not thought necessary, in view of the destiny of the majority of children, to provide a particularly developed kind of education. Revealingly, despite their critical notes, the inspectors were not on the whole very concerned with the inadequacies of primary education. Their introduction states that children are, for the most part, 'introduced to a wide range of knowledge and skills'[5] – a finding implicitly contradicted by the rest of the report, and indicative mainly of complacency.

Nor can other typical aspects of the school regime be termed progressive: the prevalence, for instance, of religious education, over and above the statutory daily act of worship:

> In four fifths of the classes children were learning about man's attempt to frame religious and moral values, and the Bible was the most common source of the material used . . . Nearly a quarter of all heads referred specifically to Christian teaching. Other heads, not exclusively from denominational schools,

emphasised equally strongly the particular Christian commitment of their schools.[6]

Corporal punishment, hardly a mark of progress, is still prevalent. Although several education authorities have now taken steps to end its use, and have, since 1982, been supported by the NUT, it is still, in most schools regarded as a necessary element of discipline. A recent indicator of grassroots teacher feeling towards it was the NUT survey of membership opinion carried out in 1979. Only 10 per cent of the branches that responded were in favour of its abolition; by contrast, 15 per cent of the branches were in favour of its use against children less than 5 years old.

In all of this, schools do not simply reflect the pressure of the labour market. They also actively sustain ideologies that perpetuate inequality. The Rampton/Swann enquiry into the education of West Indian students argued that the attitude and low expectations of teachers had a major part in the poor educational performance of students.[7] Similarly, studies have shown how 'male teachers tend to marginalise or simply ignore the female students', with consequences for the self-image and achievement of the students.[8] There is no reason to assume that working-class students fare any better, nor that most teachers have a more enlightened view of their ability and potential.

Sixty years, then, after the Labour Party's adoption of a formal programme of educational reform, English schools offer to the majority of their students an education that provides little knowledge of natural and social life, and little preparation in skills of criticism, analysis and argument. Interwoven with this failure to rise above the influence of the minimal needs of the labour market is an inability even to fully secularise the school, or to ban physical punishment from it.

Absent themes

The effect on education of economic life would be difficult for even the most militant educational tendency to deal with. However, there are measures of at least three types that seem of possible use, though none have so far been close concerns of Labour Party reformers. First, there must be efforts to resist the effects of the complex division of labour – including radical and sexual divisions – upon the school. These effects include a persistent tendency to promote stratification by criteria of 'ability' – a tendency which isolates the majority of students from forms of education which deliver some general understanding of society. This tendency arises from the inequalities of capitalism and its effects cannot be abolished by what goes on within the school. But it can in part be counteracted by the school's commitment to transmitting, in defiance of capitalism's tendency to minimise the skills and understanding of its workforce, a high level of culture, critical of such a process. To discuss such a commitment leads to consideration of a second point: to advance socialist educational interests, against the dominant tendencies of capitalism, implies the development of a conscious movement of criticism of the existing system, that combines aspirations towards a different social and educational order, with activity and organisation based upon such principles. Those who have argued equal opportunity as a strategy to benefit the working class have had no such interest.

Third, Gramsci's comment has to be remembered. 'It was right to struggle against the old school, but reforming it was not so simple as it seemed. The problem was not one of model curricula but of men.' The problem of those who staff the school, of their knowledge and biases, has not, in the perspectives of equal opportunity, been considered. Yet for any enduring effort at socialist educational advance, the question of constructing a committed movement of teachers is a crucial one.[9]

Countering privilege?

Other features of the system, being less closely related to economic necessity, are more vulnerable to a determined programme of reform. But it is difficult to be confident that they will be reformed, since Labour has so far failed to attain many of its modest policy objectives. They have foundered on, among other things, the opposition of civil service, church and law courts. The 1974 Labour Government was told by its civil servants that its proposal to remove charitable status from independent schools was fiscally impossible, and abandoned the plan. Earlier tentative proposals for the secularisation of schools and the ending of any form of church control were successfully opposed by the churches, particularly by Catholics among Labour's own supporters. Suggestions, more recently, from the Labour ILEA that the semi-autonomous existence of church schools might be ended have brought sharp resistance. Likewise, in Tameside, the government failed in an attempt to use laws of Labour's own devising to compel a Conservative education authority to become comprehensive – the Law Lords finding against it.[10]

Thus, the public schools remain, with not even their charitable status altered. As for comprehensive education – in the last full year of the Callaghan government, 1978, 70 out of 104 LEAs still had some form of selective schooling.[11] The independent sector actually expanded during Labour's last term, as direct-grant grammar schools opted out of a comprehensive system.

Some kind of comprehensive education is thus widespread, but nothing like universal. Within the comprehensive, selective principles apply. The HMI survey, *Mixed Ability Work in Comprehensive Schools*, estimated that only 2 per cent of comprehensives were completely 'unstreamed'. Nearly two-thirds had no mixed ability system of any kind, at any level.[12] Segregation by ability is the norm in the great majority of secondary schools, a situation perpetuated by a divided system of examining at $16+$, which virtually compels some form of streaming at the age of 14.

When these features are marked upon it, the map of English education becomes more forbidding. Schools' internal organisation continues *not* to be determined by principles of equal opportunity, and, combined with the patchy nature of comprehensive reorganisation, promotes in primary as well as secondary schools activities and attitudes the reverse of those that reformers intended.

Reforming history

If the reforming tradition has often underestimated the barriers to change, it has equally misrepresented its causes. The development of reform is often depicted as a series of conquests won by the forces of progress, led by the labour movement. Restricted to particular episodes, this interpretation has some truth, but as an account of the conditions that allowed state approval and confirmation of 'conquests' it is misleading. It confuses, especially, the difference between the people who were active in debating and influencing educational policy, and the policy itself. The advocates of equal opportunity, for instance, were often Labour Party members, teachers or trade unionists. But the policy for which they argued, and the terms in which they argued it were – often explicitly – concerned more with the regeneration of the British economy than with a defence of independent socialist interests.

As a corrective, then, to a rosy view of reforming history, it is useful to note some of the tendencies that have made the expansion of education and educational opportunity to some extent a necessary part of capitalist development this century.

Educational opportunity has expanded partly in reaction to two needs – one economic, the other political. The growth of white-collar employment, and the increasing complexity of the industrial division of labour, meant that the elementary school, sternly disciplined and rudimentarily provided, no longer formed an adequate preparation of the great mass of the workforce. From the 1920s onwards, under some of the most reactionary governments of the century, there was a steady growth of secondary education.[13] Likewise, the reforms of the 1950s and 1960s in secondary schools were motivated not so much by a yearning to deliver education to all, as by two different types of economic requirement, between which the more intelligent educational reports were careful to distinguish:

> The rapidity of technological change presents an exciting challenge for those who can qualify themselves as scientists, technologists and technicians. The numbers of these produced by the schools have risen rapidly and will continue to do so. But they will remain a minority of the working population. For the remainder, the advent of a technological age creates different needs – to be able to comprehend something of the language of science and technology; to be at home in a world of machines; and to be able to adapt to a rapidly changing environment. There may be less need in the future of 'skill' in the old-fashioned sense of the word; what will be needed . . . will be that quality that can best be described as 'general mechanical intelligence'.[14]

Changes in the curriculum and organisation of schools made an attempt to match both types of need. Comprehensives were initially supported as a means both of producing the minority qualified in new technological skills, and an adaptable 'semi-skilled' majority.[15] It is not so much the generous pulse of egalitarian reform that can be heard behind Crowther's prescriptions as the ticking of economic calculation.

The expansion of education has had an equally functional political basis. Reform has at crucial times been prompted by the imperative – as in 1870 – to 'educate our masters'; or – as in 1918 – to halt what the Secretary of the Board of Education called the spread of 'dangerous class antagonisms'; or – as in 1945 – to deliver a package of reform so as to avert greater political tumult. (As Quintin Hogg put it, reform was the alternative to revolution.) The elementary school was thoroughly unfitted for a major role in the reproduction of a citizenry which accepted its place in a representative democracy with tolerance and loyalty. The harshness of its discipline, the blatant class discrimination embodied in its penury and the mechanical way in which it imposed, rather than fostered, ideologies of loyalty to King and Empire, all threw it out of step with what were seen as contemporary needs.

Reform does not equal modernisation

It is with concerns such as these that reforms of the school have often been occupied. Yet it would be wrong to assume that they have reflected economic or political 'need' in an impeccably rational way. One of the more interesting features of twentieth-century educational policy is the way in which it has failed to create a school system adequate to the tasks of technical and political modernisation. The Fisher Act of 1918, the Hadow Report of 1926, the Spens Report of 1937 and the McNair Report of 1944 all criticised the absence of a scientific and technical bias in the English system. All stressed it was vital to future economic success. Yet none produced an adequate remodelling of the system – complaint followed by inaction is the characteristic pattern of educational policy. Thus the 1918 Education Act provided for a never-to-be-implemented scheme of compulsory post-school education. And thus the famous tripartite reshaping of education after 1944 was in reality almost wholly bipartite: technical schools, the supposed third branch of the system, never amounted to more than 5 per cent of the secondary school total. Nor did the reforms of the 1960s produce a successful modernisation.

In 1975 the OECD passed judgement on fifty years of this kind of planning: 'We miss [in the DES] a balanced analysis of persisting and new trends in society, in technological development and the role of the state, and of the place of education and science in the process of production.'[16] In its report, the OECD quoted the DES reply to its criticisms – that there existed 'resistances and frictions in the system' which meant that 'major changes of direction and pace can be achieved only slowly'. The DES did not specify what these 'resistances' were, but, during the 'Great Debate' which was opened in the following year, it made clear that the educational policy of the past had erred in encouraging schools to prepare students for their 'social' rather than their 'economic' role.[17] The criticism was accurate. Educational planning had never, of course, formally rejected the role of schools in preparing students for work. But it had, consistently, perceived the task of modernising education through the medium of an increase in educational opportunity. The latter, except in such exceptions as the Crowther Report, was seen as the key to the former. But this would have been true only if there had existed in the schools a strong practical–technical orientation. In the absence of such a bias, equal opportunity would tend only, at the top end of the scale, to deliver students to an academic type of education, and at its lower end, to neglect training in the attitudes and skills appropriate to the majority of the workforce. Although the occasional report like Crowther took a clear-sighted and economically based view of educational purpose, and though no influential opinion was in explicit disagreement with Crowther's approach, in practice policy has been elaborated differently. The bias of reform has been towards the achievement of social peace and harmony between the classes, an aim whose educational correlate has been a rhetoric of individual self-development. The reformers of the 1920s intended that a new curriculum should create 'a national unity, linking together the mental life of all classes by experiences hitherto . . . the privileges of a limited section'.[18] Similar aims and worries can be found in the major post-war reports; though, since class conflict was then less acute, they are expressed in less sharply political terms than those of their predecessors. Plowden, Bullock and Newsom all share a concern to mitigate social differences between classes, and to draw an intractable working class into a unified national experience. This persistent cultural, even ethical, stress affected policy for most of the post-war period and, as the DES hinted, was in conflict with an approach that wished to prioritise a strengthening of the links between schooling and employment.

Two limitations

The reforming movement, then, has encountered limits of two kinds. As a strategy for working-class advance, it has not achieved thoroughgoing reforms; a rhetoric of opportunity has done little to diminish the effects on education of economic life, and coexists with strong enclaves of privilege and large areas of backwardness. It is, moreover, a strategy without organic links with those whose interests it claims to represent. Nor, though, can it be an adequate instrument of state policy, since the occupation of the centre stage by equal opportunity has displaced precise consideration of what the OECD called 'the place of education . . . in the process of production',[19] while the influence of considerations of social harmony, traditional concern of the English intelligentsia, inhibited the development of a technical bias in the school.

The following two chapters look at the origins and development of these weaknesses.

2
Progressive education

Progressive education is normally associated with activity in the classroom, and has thus been thought of mainly in connection with curriculum and with teaching method. This chapter tries to consider progressive education more widely, to look not just at its pedagogy, but at its context, motivating philosophy and strategies for gaining influence – as well as examining the modifications that these have undergone in the course of time.

It is useful to consider the history of progressive education, partly because such an approach can explain some features of the modern education system, and also because the pristine ideas of progressive education were presented and argued for in ways that reveal more about its underpinning assumptions than any later development. It is also only over time that the results of the dialogue between progressive education and a state system that helps service a particular division of labour become apparent, provoking the question: what was there in the nature of progressivism that allowed its assimilation, despite its many initially critical positions, into the education system, and effected a corresponding modification of its original beliefs?

Origins of progresive education

The influence of progressive education can be traced back to the period before and immediately following the First World War, when the ideas of the progressives provided the only available coherent programme for a modernisation of education which was increasingly seen as a priority by governments and industry. Modernisation was a need related to important changes not only in production but in social life. The process of concentration of capital increased the size of the average firm, and eliminated many small firms. Changes in the production process, and the rapid growth of new industries in chemicals and electrical engineering, eradicated old skills and made new technical demands. Within industry, and with the growth of public administration, arose a more complex division of labour, with a growth of white-collar work. Associated urbanisation broke up old patterns of social life, and created new forms of political and social organisation, and new kinds of leisure. These trends not only gave rise to new demands on the part of industry and of other forms of employment, but were also disruptive of established political order and social control. Some kind of intervention beyond the merely repressive was necessary to create and maintain social unity. Political integration of the working class and state intervention in social life were two such responses.

In the older capitalist countries, such as Britain, these processes had been under way for some time. But it cannot be said that state intervention in English education was of an advanced kind. Little in the state schools reflected awareness of the changed conditions. Secondary (that is, grammar) schools, taking their model from the private sector, were academic rather than technical in character. Elementary schooling concentrated on social control through repressive discipline, nationalist ritual and moral instruction. 'Industry, self-control, perseverance, self-sacrifice, purity, duty, unselfishness' were the behavioural objectives stipulated by the Board of Education in the early 1900s.[1] After the First World War, some forms of nationalism were actually revived, under the stimulus of the Communist menace. Such was Empire Day:

A fortnight in advance of Empire Day we were asked to teach our classes Rule Britannia . . . We were given outline maps of the world and the pupils coloured the British possessions red . . . Then came the day. Britannia led the way and was guarded by boys dressed as soldiers . . . Rule Britannia was sung by the school and the head gave a little speech between each verse: 'We are all proud of our flag because wherever it waves there is justice and freedom. In many countries there were slaves but the coming of the Union Jack meant the abolition of slavery'. Enter William Wilberforce, who was duly saluted.[2]

Despite the fears of the rulers, little happened in the schools to counterbalance these rituals. Hence the comment of one socialist newspaper when a 'Seditious Teachings Bill' was moved in Parliament: 'We hope they will not have as much trouble as we think they will in finding such schools.'[3]

It was becoming clear, though, that the system was ineffective, and that the country's international position dictated change. If 'never again' meant anything to the Parliament of 1918, it meant a determination to regain superiority over rival nations. In 1914, in most of the characteristic products of the second wave of the industrial revolution, British industry lagged well behind the technical and commercial successes of Germany and the USA. The discrepancy was notorious; a tradition had developed that critically contrasted the British and German systems of scientific and technical training.[4] The reforms of the 1918 Education Act responded by promising to raise the school-leaving age to 14, and to make compulsory part-time education to the age of 18.

There were, then, a number of economic reasons for change. But what gave the demand for reform its special edge was the political crisis – the acute class conflict – of the post-war years. The tempering of class conflict was a priority of reform. 'We have repeatedly stated', wrote *The Times Educational Supplement*, 'that the new franchise and the new education are supplementary things. Without education, Bolshevism, or syndicalism run mad, indicate the unconscious goal.'[5] In the same spirit, the Directorate of Intelligence had noted, in 1920, not the extent of seditious teaching in schools (as indicated, it was pretty minimal) but rather the strength of the workers' self-education movement, which had developed in the spaces left by the state system:

Class prejudice and ignorance of elementary economics has a firmer grip on the working class of the country than ever before ... The great need for the moment is instruction and unfortunately almost the only agency is the Labour Colleges.[6]

The President of the Board of Education himself had pleaded the virtues of a broader education for the working class that 'could dispel the hideous clouds of class suspicion, and soften the asperities of faction'.[7]

The old education, then, would not do. What alternatives, other than those of militant socialism, were there? Within the existing system, there were very few. The prevailing academic model of secondary education offered little that could reshape the spirit of mass education. There had been some limited encouragement of 'higher elementary schools' which did provide scientific and technical training, but, by 1916, there were only thirty-one such schools in England and Wales.[8] The renewal of English education thus depended on sources outside the existing system: in American or European – or native – versions of progressive education. But no source provided ideas that could, simply and unproblematically, modernise education. Each introduced currents of criticism and dissent into English education.

Dewey

The most impressive writings on progressive education are those of the American, John Dewey. His work registers the implications of social and economic change for the school with a clarity that few have matched. Other accounts of his ideas[9] have pointed to the lack of realism of his major assumption, 'that occupational roles in capitalist society are best filled by individuals who have achieved the highest possible levels of personal development'.[10] They correctly argue that this flaw vitiates his whole work. Here, though, I want to stress two other features of his writing. First, that it is one of the few coherent attempts to develop a distinctively modern educational practice. Second, that it is in many respects critical of industrial capitalism. The second feature is largely a result of the first – an uneasy combination of modernisation and social criticism which typifies progressive education.

Dewey's early work tried to register the importance for the school of the new world market, of industrialisation and political democracy, and of the scientific analysis of human behaviour. For him, the task of the school was not simply to train appropriately skilled workers; he would not have been impressed with many of the themes of the 'Great Debate'. It was the school's role, rather, to create the conditions in which the entire necessary fabric of modern society could be reproduced. The contemporary school did not do this. 'In the school-room the motive and the cement of social organisation are alike wanting.'[11] To provide the cement, the immediate imperatives of industry – those of the 'soul-less monotony of the machine' – must be rejected. Education had to develop a culture appropriate to the many-sided demands of the new type of society. Its task was:

> to discover the factors of scientific and social importance in present-day industry and in a common democratic life, and to utilise them for educational purposes, as was done by our spiritual progenitors in the work of selecting the factors of value in a non-industrial society.[12]

Dewey's aim of an education able to transmit an all-round understanding of economic and political processes was not, nor seems likely to be, achieved. Dewey was aware of this. He noted that the modern division of labour fragmented the activity and consciousness of its workers. Instead of following through an extended piece of work, which might point towards a complete understanding of a production process, the worker's understanding of labour had become limited to a purely technical knowledge of a particular circumscribed task. Nor was productive work complemented by any understanding of the social context of production.

In response, Dewey developed ideas for an education that would compensate for both kinds of limitation. This meant, on the one hand, bringing labour into the schools – introducing 'practical operations' such as weaving and spinning, with the aim of 'supplying the child with a genuine motive' that 'exacts personal responsibility and trains the child in relation to the physical realities of life'. On the other hand, lest this become just another form of vocational education, Dewey emphasised that the work should be 'liberalised throughout by its translation into historic and social values'.[13]

His proposals thus combined criticism of industry, preparation for some of its demands, and compensation for its effects on the social order. Work in the school of Dewey aimed to produce the moral, social and scientific understandings that modern society required, yet which were the opposite of the tendencies produced in the labour process of that society. To serve society, education had to criticise some of its most fundamental processes. But if education tended to subvert industry, it was itself far more thoroughly undermined in return. Every step that Dewey took to deliver an insight into the workings of productive life was counterbalanced by the orientation of post-school society, in which the production process was mystified and the worker excluded from understanding. Dewey's formula was not capable of solving this problem. The kind of labour he wished to introduce into the school was, literally, *manu*facture, typical of the early stages of the industrial revolution, rather than of the more advanced stage that Dewey intended his school to serve. It could teach physical skills, but could offer no insight into the complexity of the modern industrial process. Nor could it give an understanding of the social relations between the classes involved in production. His attempt to translate labour into its 'historic and social values', which would then be discussed in the classroom, substituted for these wider connections and, as Dewey later realised, could not replace them.

In 1926, after visiting the Soviet Union, his identification of problem and solution became much sharper:

> I do not see how any honest educational reformer in western countries can deny that the greatest practical obstacle in the way of the introduction into schools of that connexion with social life that he regards as desirable, is the great part played by personal competition and the desire for private profit in our economic life. This fact makes it almost necessary that . . . school activities should be protected from social contacts and connexions instead of being organised to create them. The Russian educational situation is enough to convert one to the idea that only in a society based on the co-operative principle can the ideals of educational reformers be carried into operation.[14]

As in American theory, the Russians centred the school 'about the study of human work in its connexion on one side with natural materials and energies and on the other with social and political history and institutions'.[15] The Russians 'acknowledge an initial indebtedness to American theory' but 'criticise many of the projects employed in our schools as casual and trivial, because they do not belong to any general social aim, nor have any definite social consequences'.[16]

In his reflections on Russia, Dewey began to consider not just the technical but the social division of labour. He saw that the relation to each other of the classes involved in the labour process created pressures of competition and mystification which excluded the subordinate class from any overall knowledge. He also suggested some of the ways in which this tendency could be opposed, through transforming the school, not into a workshop, but into a centre for the investigation of social and economic life. Yet this remained a suggestion only. In practice, Dewey's response to the barriers imposed by 'personal competition and the desire for private profit' was less to overturn them than to retreat. His work on the Soviet Union ends with the argument that the isolation of the school is preferable to its involvement in a productive life dominated by the profit motive. He thus followed a convoluted path, typical, too, of later progressives; to be thoroughly modern, the school must go out into the world, yet the laws of that world discouraged any such venture. To maintain its critical attitude the school had therefore to keep its distance from production, unless it wished only to be a vocational instrument. A retreat like this inhibited the project of modernising education.

The Europeans

Dewey's attempt to construct a systematic basis for a distinctively modern education distinguished him from European progressives. Like him, they were critical of industrialisation. But their reaction was more deeply tinged with an objection to industrialism as such, regardless of the class relations it was based on. This response was linked to a criticism of society made in the name of values seen to be stifled or distorted in the school system. Whereas Dewey defined educational purpose in terms of the individual's integration into a modern society, the Europeans laid greater stress on 'self-realisation' and the inner growth of the individual. If they talked of community and co-operation, it was not in a way that was related to specific contemporary situations. If Dewey's stress was on the need to match education to the latest stage of economic and social development, theirs was on the 'needs of the child'. This faith, in the early post-war years, was central to a complex of beliefs which included yearnings for social justice, concern for the future of civilisation, theories scientific and sentimental of child development, and an imprecise recognition of the needs of a new stage of society. The principles of European progressivism were summed up by one of its leading promoters, the New Education Fellowship:

> The essential aim of all education is to prepare the child to seek and realise in his own life the supremacy of the spirit . . . Education should respect the child's individuality . . . The studies should give free play to the child's innate interests . . . Selfish competition must disappear from education and be replaced by the co-operation which teaches the child to put himself at the service of his community . . . The New Education fits the child to become not only a citizen capable of doing his duties to his neighbours, his nation and humanity at large, but also a human being conscious of his own personal dignity.[17]

There were a number of reasons why this apparently incongruous ideology came forward as the means by which the state school could be regenerated. The old system was manifestly not working. Its faults were seen as ones of educational method; remoteness from industrial need and classroom didacticism were thought to be closely related. Thus a system that offered itself as an approach to the latter problem could easily be seen as the solution to the former as well. There was no alternative project of modernisation, and no existing current in the system which could take up, transform and utilise some of the progressive insights, in the context of a plan for the technical modernisation of the school. Indeed, it was here that the progressive ideas seemed to be useful. In particular, their attention to the practical activity of the student seemed useful in dealing not only with vocational education, but also with the problem of motivation. In this context, 'self-government' and co-operation were attractive concepts. They stood less for an ideal of students' rights than for the voluntary submission of the student to the behavioural requirements of social unity, and for the participation of the student in the practices that sustained it. During the General Strike, the newspaper of the NUT congratulated teachers on their successful efforts to encourage co-operation:

> In the schools today teachers pride themselves on the habits of self-government which they are inculcating in their pupils; the fact that strike meetings and processions were conducted all over the country without conflict with the police . . . shows that the self-governing instinct is being strongly developed.[18]

As a means of social control, 'self-government' was more effective than Empire Day processions.

The concern of the European progressives with the individual and with the creation of individually felt communal values was also congenial to an important English intellectual tradition – a not-necessarily-radical fear of the disintegrative forces of industrialism and political democracy, and a concern to find some system of values on which social unity could be based. In its English form, progressive education took on many of the features of this tradition. But its immediate appeal was that of a crusade. To achieve its ends, the old school had to be swept away. Community must be based on consent, not force. Classroom relations must be humanised; the teacher must take on a creative, not a repressive role. These themes had a resonance. The embattled teacher-innovator became a progressive hero. New projects were taken up wholescale – when the 'Dalton Plan' for individualised project work was written up in the *TES*, there were more than 2,000 applications for further details within a week.[19] The progressive movement set up its own organisations – schools, conferences, international committees – to exemplify its principles and win converts. It suffered its own martyrdoms. Yet within a few years, by the 1930s, its momentum had slowed down, so that its experiments were fewer, its critiques less sharp and its existence quite tolerable to the established order. What allowed this transformation?

Progressives and state policy

Part of the answer can be seen in the way that some of the progressive insights were utilised by the agencies of state reform and fed back, greatly changed, into the education system.

Progressivism in England showed little awareness that the chief principle of mass schooling was the preparation of students for a limited political and economic role. Because its educational concepts were not related to such an understanding, they were capable of being 'de-radicalised' and presented as aspects of a programme for a modernisation of the school which would leave its basic functions unaffected. This was the case with two of its central ideas: its stress on 'practical activity' and its 'anti-bookishness'.

The attack on bookishness began as a means of understanding rote-learning. 'Bookishness' was a term used to describe a type of education that subjected the child to a tyranny of irrelevant and uncomprehended fact, and that was thus unable either to assist self-development or to deliver an understanding of modern society. 'Practical activity' was suggested as an alternative principle. In Dewey's thought, it was associated with the attempt to link the school to political and productive life and to convert it into an institution which defied the expectations of industry.

But when these ideas were taken up by the Board of Education's Consultative Committee in 1926, their meanings were altered. The Committee – on which several prominent progressives sat – was alarmed at the social wastage created by the treatment of the working-class child at elementary school. Rote-learning and neglect of the child's interests were criticised and several progressive concepts apparently endorsed. But when the Committee recommended a connection between school and local environment, to quicken the interest of the learner, this was not to bring about any general or critical understanding of that environment, but merely to offer a more appropriate introduction to life as a manual worker. The curriculum should be brought into relation with local conditions because 'with a lengthening of schooling . . . it is now possible to give the instruction of older pupils a useful trend towards the occupations which await them'.[20] In the context of an unchallenged segregated system, which kept mental and manual labour firmly separated, a stress on practical activity in the elementary school amounted to endorsing the ineluctable destiny of most of the students. Likewise, the rejection of bookishness came to mean the rejection not only of rote-learning, but also of any effort to achieve high intellectual standards in mass education.

Thus, whereas Dewey's ideas and those of English progressivism employed similar terms, the meaning of these terms, as employed in their different contexts, varied considerably. The connection between school and 'life' was in one case intended to create an understanding of social processes, but in the other only to serve as a new form of motivation and a more practical preparation for working life. This deradicalised employment of its central concepts became a characteristic of the relationship of English progressivism to state reform. It was a parcel of loosely connected ideas and practices which combined criticism of the status quo with support of techniques that could be used to regenerate, but not to fundamentally transform, mass education; thus its equivocal role: at once the challenger of many features of the school, and a means by which the school adapted itself, the better to survive. It is arguable that no form of progressive practice has yet escaped the contradictions of such a role.

Philosophies

This failure can also be in part explained by the philosophical outlook of progressive education. The most immediately striking characteristic of the English progressives is their background in various forms of religious belief, in which the child often figured as a symbol of uncorrupted human potential. Edmond Holmes, Inspector of Schools, and author of the seminal *What Is and What Should Be*, was a buddhist. Homer Lane, founder of the 'Little Commonwealth' educational community, believed himself to be the only man who really understood the teachings of Jesus Christ.[21] The New Education Fellowship was inspired and organised by Theosophists. Margaret McMillan, originator of the nursery-education movement, was a Christian Socialist. 'Listening to her,' wrote one of her biographers, 'textile workers were made aware of their children not as "doffers" or "little piecers" but as heirs of the ages, lilies of the field and lambs of God.'[22] Maria Montessori, an Italian catholic, much taken up in England, interpreted the old education as a kind of Calvary: 'Thus the child repeats the Passion of Christ . . . The child's hands and feet are fastened to the desk by stern looks which hold them as motionless as the nails of the cross in the feet of Christ.'[23] For them, the learning activity of the child typified the way in which humans gain knowledge of the world, through their innate, spontaneous, non-reflective capacities. There was a great stress on the release of mental energies, so that they could freely shape the world. As one successful progressive put it: 'We stand on the position that nothing good enters the world except in and through the free activities of individual men and women, and that educational practice must be shaped to accord with this truth.'[24]

There was thus a tendency to concentrate on the activity involved in the acquisition of knowledge, without a concern for those social and natural factors that limit free activity and themselves need to be known. Not only the activity of learning, but also the character of what is known is important. The progressives avoided this latter issue, and begged the educational questions that it posed: what should be learned about reality, what were the necessary methods and components of knowledge? Such a disability contributed to progressivism's failure to develop a consistent alternative to mainstream education; it could criticise the regime of the school, but not, in any detail, the kind of knowledge it offered of modern society.

Politics

The political strategy of the progressives also helped make their adoption of a weightier critique more unlikely. They combined an avoidance of directly political debate on how the desired education system could be constructed and controlled, with a practical orientation towards the immediately available sources of influence and patronage. A. S. Neill offered this interpretation of the 'Labour teacher's task':

It is for the spiritual in life, not the political and economic. It is his mission to give his pupils absolute freedom to be wise and good . . . This he can only do if he believes in children more than he believes in politics and economics. To abolish the East End of London is a psychological rather than an economic problem.[25]

Consequently there was little advice he could offer on political activity. 'Rebels in the NUT? Here I have nothing to advise.'[26] Much later, in *Summerhill*, he explained the logic of his position:

> If I tried to reform society by action, society would kill me as a public danger ... Hating compromise as I do, I have to compromise here, realising that my primary job is not the reformation of society, but the bringing of happiness to some few children.[27]

Both the outlines of a desire for social change and the quietist conclusions are familiar features of progressive education, whose radicals found no political strategy to complement their educational aspirations. By contrast, Neill's contemporary, the French progressive Celestin Freinet, had an intensely political conception of how the change he wanted would be brought about. 'It is the mass of educators whom we must mobilise for our fight', he wrote[28] – and meant it. The radical educational movement he founded is still in active existence. Noting comparable existed or exists in England. The characteristic forms of organisation were the conference, the little magazine, the brave but isolated experiment. Objective conditions alone cannot explain this; progressive activists, even, like Neill, of the left, were reluctant to organise a fight for their ideas in every available forum, or to develop an explicit programme, together with the strategies and the alliances to achieve it. Whereas Freinet was convinced that the base for the kind of education he wanted could only be 'a people conscious of its historical mission',[29] the English progressives sought no allies – except in a local or accidental way – among the people. Links, of a sort, with the labour movement did exist. Several progressives joined the non-elected experts on the Labour Party's Advisory Committee on Education (ACE), which had an important influence on policy development.

The leaders of the TUC, guided by the ACE, were impressed by many aspects of progressive education. In particular, it was attractive because it seemed to raise the status of 'handwork' (manual labour),[30] because it was opposed to the well-remembered barbarities of the elementary-school regime, and because it offered, in its concern for the human personality as a whole, a much broader and more interesting education for working-class children. The welcome that the TUC extended to the progressives, though, was not accompanied by any sustained or critical dialogue. There were few connections, too, between the more radical movements for politically independent working-class education and the progressives. Such sympathy that did exist was not translated into an alliance which could fight for common educational purposes. Progressivism went its separate, unmodified way, the subject of some working-class interest, but in no sense an organic part of a radical educational movement.

Yet progressives were not devoid of strategy. Their search for 'happiness for some few children' led them to use whatever method of advancement came to hand. This meant, at first, private sponsorship, and later the benevolent offices of the state. In these quests, they were quite successful, especially in areas of education that were innovative, met a clear need and seemed remote enough from class conflict to be politically safe.

Maria Montessori, for instance, upon her arrival in England in 1919, was fêted at the Savoy, with the President of the Board of Education at the head of the table.[31] In the same year, Margaret McMillan received the Queen at her nursery in Deptford. 'If the first lady in the land will come from Buckingham Palace to see my poor palace, it means that she has faith in us and the work must go on', said McMillan, who later became an occasional visitor to the Palace.[32] Other progressives, though not receiving such high patronage, looked to (necessarily) unconventional landowners and industrialists for funds and support. These ventures were followed by a quest for official recognition, which was often granted. Susan Isaacs, for instance, who had managed an experimental private primary school at Cambridge, and Margaret McMillan, were in demand as witnesses to government committees. Others, such as Percy Nunn, achieved high academic status. It was only those committed to fairly threatening practices – student self-organisation or Freudian psychology – who aroused much fear and retaliation. Neill's school, for instance, was never recognised by the Inspectorate; Homer Lane was hounded by a Home Office enquiry and was eventually expelled from the country under the Aliens Act.[33]

The lack of hostility on the part of the central state did not mean that progressive teachers were welcomed everywhere with open arms. There were many cases of local conflict and persecution; but the overall trend was one of selective acceptance.

Progressivism in a tripartite system

The first wave of progressive education contained tendencies that weakened its ability to resist the influence of a system geared to preparing students for their unequal future roles. As a result, progressivism, compliantly, took on a different form according to the part of the system in which it happened to be operating: it had one function in grammar schools, quite another elsewhere.

Inter-war reports from the Board of Education's Consultative Committee endorsed many aspects of progressive education, while at the same time they reinforced the division between secondary (grammar) schools and the rest. As long as the secondaries were unchallenged at the pinnacle of the state system, and as long as they were dominated by an academic model of education, it was inevitable that practical education would be associated with the lower end of the system, and would be more a preparation for manual labour than part of a plan for the transmission of a general knowledge of society.

Progressive education, rather than presenting a unifying model of education, itself developed divergent 'academic' and 'practical' tendencies. On the one hand, its concern with 'interests arising from the social and industrial environment of the pupils'[34] was bound fairly closely to the 'instruction of the older pupils' in 'the occupations which await them' and was biased towards limited forms of knowledge. On the other hand, progressivism's wider cultural concerns were incorporated into the anti-industrial culture-criticism which had influence in many secondary schools.

There were trends in progressive education which, though critical of the private ownership of capital, were not hostile to industry as such. But, in England at least, these – the tendencies of a Dewey – were outweighed by others which saw industry as a spiritually degrading and culturally divisive force. Whereas for Dewey 'creativity' and 'industry' were in many senses compatible, in England they were seen as antithetical: an attitude that affected not just the occasional progressive thinker, but even the character of official educational reports – such as the Consultative Committee's Spens Report on Secondary Education (1938). The report begins with the familiar list of complaints about the weaknesses of English technical education. It points out the unfortunate results of separating 'the concept of a general education' from 'the idea of a technical or quasi-technical education': although the secondary-school population had increased fivefold since the beginning of the century, there had been no complementary development of a technical culture in the schools.

Spens's criticisms went further. The secondary curriculum was out of date. It was over-concerned with university entrance, and took little account of the interests of the pupil. But with the broadening of criticism came a shift of emphasis. Technical education has little importance in Spens's conclusions, where, in so much as 'practical' activity and understanding are discussed, it is in terms of a concept of 'activity' that had increasingly come to mean the creative activity of the mind alone. By collapsing technical education into 'creativity' in this way, Spens is prevented from suggesting solutions to the crisis he earlier described. Instead, the report recommends that the culture of the school should be reshaped around one subject – English:

> English represents a line of activity . . . which has played an essential part in the evolution of the human spirit . . . We think that the school itself should adopt a unifying principle in its curriculum, and we recommend that it be found in the teaching of English.[35]

The stress was the same as that of much progressive writing. English was the most accessible medium of creativity and thus, as Nunn argued, 'of school studies, literature is from the present standpoint the most important'.[36] In the context of secondary education, this meant putting at the centre of the curriculum a critical social philosophy, which saw literature as a bulwark against the disorders of the industrial revolution and its culture. In the 1930s this critical faith found its most cogent expression in the magazine *Scrutiny*, associated with F. R. Leavis. Another of the magazine's editors, Denys Thompson, tried with some success to build an organisation of teachers of English committed to cultural criticism and to a belief that 'education, a potentially "humanising" activity, was at present complicit with "the economic process"; that it should be reformed as a centre of opposition to the latter'.[37] This position was not, of course, hegemonic across the school system; its influence was localised in one department of a particular sector of education. Nevertheless, over the next three decades, the influence was a real one, occupying a central place in the most influential sector of state schooling, and ensuring not only that technical education enjoyed no dominance, but also that one of the main ways in which educational purpose was consciously formulated by teachers had a strong socially critical element.

In other respects, too, progressivism was modified by the overall needs of the institution in which it operated. After 1944, it found a place in the secondary modern school, where its emphasis on the needs of the child rather than those of the academic subject became identified with a second-class education whose recipients were relieved of the necessity to take public examinations. A Ministry of Education pamphlet described this type of education as 'a good all-round secondary education, not focussed primarily on the subjects of the school curriculum, but developing out of the interests of the child'.[38] Once again, progressive methods were seen as a way of producing the attitudes appropriate to the self-governing citizen and the adaptable worker. As the Ministry put it: 'The ultimate criterion of the quality of education is . . . above all the nature of [the student's] attitudes and his behaviour towards those with whom he works and plays.'[39]

The techniques and values of progressivism were thus common to many areas of English schooling – though in a form subservient to the tripartite system. When progressive educational ideas were re-utilised, on a grander scale, in the 1960s, it was in a form still heavily affected by non-academic stresses of the kind made by the Ministry pamphlet. This was not to be altered by the spread from the grammar school to 'mass' education of some of the cultural concerns encouraged by the Spens report.

A new wave

We should, before considering English progressivism in its more modern forms, note several particular features of its developing traditions: its concentration on the needs of the child, and its assumption that social benefits would flow from such a concentration; its tendency towards anti-industrialism – or, at least, its lack of interest in precise problems of economic development; its related inability to outline a body of knowledge appropriate to modern society; its political strategy, which rested on its incorporation into projects of state reform; and finally, its inability to link its conceptions of the 'self-activity' of the student to forms of self-activity which could assist in developing a more complete understanding of social processes by allowing some participation in political and economic life. These tendencies, it will be argued, continue to exist in more modern forms of progressive education.

Between 1945 and 1960 there was a continued growth of educational spending, and a slow movement towards comprehensive education. But it was not until the 1960s that there was a renewed spurt of educational reform and a new impetus given to progressive education. The context of the sudden leap forward was the conviction – held by the Conservative Government of 1959–64 and more firmly, at first, by the governments of Harold Wilson (1964–70) – that the British economy, in order to compete on a world scale, needed a greater degree of state intervention in economic planning and a thorough overhaul of the social infrastructure of the country. One aspect of the overhaul was to be the expansion of further and higher education, with many more students being given the opportunity to receive it. This in turn implied a utilisation of as-yet-untapped human resources: those children excluded in the past from grammar-school education, and thus (since secondary modern schools were discouraged from entering students for many public examinations) from most systems of academic qualification. These objectives lay behind the growth of comprehensive education.

It is important to note that the drive towards modernisation was thought to depend upon an increase in opportunity. It was in this context that the concerns of progressive education were re-employed to secure the integration of all children in a framework of equal opportunity. Progressivism seemed to be the necessary complement of comprehensive education, since it was concerned not merely with questions of access, but with the dismantling of the cultural barriers that were thought to come between working-class children and educational success. As the Newsom Report put it, its target was to be 'those pupils whose abilities are artificially depressed by environmental and linguistic handicaps'.[40] It was assumed that child-centred education of some kind offered the best approach to such a 'problem'.

To those teachers trained in the 1960s and 1970s, such a priority may seem to be a natural and automatic one (so much have we been saturated in the concerns of those times). But it is necessary to underline what is, in economic terms, its strangeness: it discussed educational objectives not primarily in terms of output into the economy, but in terms of the cultural development of individuals and groups. It is one of the great unprovens of educational reform that the latter aim offers the best means of meeting economic requirements. Its prominence, nevertheless, in policy-making, makes it possible to speak of the strong influence, at that time, of progressive objectives in state educational planning, or, rather, in the approaches that were developed by semi-autonomous state agencies. For, before discussing progressive objectives in more detail, it is important to outline the forms of government and central control over educational policy in the 1960s, and to emphasise their looseness and the degree of autonomy that they involved.

The main agency of curriculum development was the Schools Council, set up in 1964. It was a major institution, free from direct control. Between the wars, the curriculum had been influenced chiefly by notes of guidance, direct from the Board of Education. In the early 1960s, the Ministry of Education had attempted another initiative of this kind, through a 'Curriculum Policy Group'. The setting up of the Schools Council was a defeat for this centralising tendency at the hands of a coalition of LEAs and teaching unions, which secured strong representation on the new body.[41] For the next decade, the Council was the main forum of debate, and source of initiatives, concerning the curriculum. The curriculum, notoriously, was not a matter for government policy: one Minister of Education spoke of it as a 'secret garden'. This was part of the context of comprehensive reorganisation: the spectacle, extraordinary in retrospect, of a major reform of secondary education being introduced without any centralised attempt to determine the curricular objectives of the new school.

Officially sponsored dreams . . .

Such a situation would have been less serious had the Schools Council, or government-commissioned reports, concerned themselves with such objectives, from a viewpoint that took account of economic and technical need. But this was not the case. Whereas Crowther at the end of the 1950s did try to determine educational objectives in the light of manpower need, the reports of the 1960s did not. Instead, both the Schools Council and the major reports such as Newsom (1963) had a bias towards moral and cultural questions, which they related, often, to individual development. The aim of education, said one Schools Council publication, was 'to help students find within themselves the resources that alone can help them live at ease in the changing world'.[42] The school 'must be devoted to the opportunities needed to master the arts of civilised life'.[43] The same tone characterised the discussions, in 1963, that preceded the setting up of the CSE exam. Its main virtue lay in the fact that it was not really an exam: 'The CSE is neither a selection test, nor a competition for a limited number of prizes.'[44] It was hoped that exam boards would 'do all they can to secure a wide understanding amongst parents and users of the certificate of the limitations of public exams'. Instead, what was seen as the new exams' most positive characteristic was their 'freshness and vitality'. It was hoped that they would 'reflect and not inhibit the originality of the work being done in the schools'. Like the statements, quoted above, made by the Ministry of Education in the immediate post-war years, the document and the new exams are content with a non-academic curriculum. But for the most part the document lacks the patronising tone of earlier official announcements: it is now a positive virtue to be outside the straitjacket of 'O' Level, in a realm pervaded by 'freshness and originality'. But the excited language reveals, more than it covers up, the continued separation of mass education from academic education. It could be added that the CSE document also fails to suggest, except vaguely, the means by which the new exam could lead the curriculum in the direction required by economic development. Technology and applied science are not discussed.

A similar contrast between excited rhetoric and prosaic reality is shown in other documents of the time. The Newsom Report, *Half our Future*, identified the 50-or-so per cent of secondary students then educated largely outside a framework of equal opportunity as a key economic resource. Crowther, five years previously, had made a crucial distinction between skills in the workforce and its adaptability; the need for the latter would grow, but this would require no overall increase in the level of skills of the workforce. Newsom, however, assumed the opposite. The reorganisation of industry and other sources of employment, in an expected context of continuing economic growth, would raise the level of skill required and in the process necessitate an education that developed individual qualities to a new height. The view was repeated more forcefully elsewhere. 'We can afford free men and we need them', stated one of the best-received progressive texts of the 1960s, Charity James's *Young Lives at Stake.* 'In a scientific age, an elite culture is a dead one; to be effective today, a society requires an inclusive culture in which scientific attitudes are widespread.'[45] This type of equation between economic and cultural development freed its authors from the need to answer some of the main questions posed by economic development: how was a layer of skilled technicians to be developed; how could a positive attitude be created in the workforce to economic modernisation, to the need for increased mobility and to the breaking down of old patterns of occupation and community? Perhaps, in a situation of economic decline, the resources did not exist that would have allowed successful answers to be made to these problems. But it cannot be argued that the English school was consistently orientated towards identifying either problem or solution.

. . . and realistic expectations

A second major concern of Newsom was the culture of working-class youth. Like most educational reports, it was happier dwelling on this than on economic issues. Newsom helped place the 'problem' of culture at the centre of educational debate. Reports of the 1920s, such as the Newbolt Report on the teaching of English,[46] had been anxious about an alleged insurrectionary mood in the working class, and had advocated its education in the spirit of a national culture as a means of allaying class antagonism. Newsom's attitude was less one of immediate alarm than of dismay at the intractability of working-class youth. They seemed to exist within a different system of values, hostile to what the school offered them. The picture, touched up from literary sources, was of a deprived and self-depriving class, badly in need of sweetness and light:

Here [in the slums] the so-called problem families tend to congregate. Life in these localities appears to be confused and disorganised. In and about the squalid streets and narrow courts, along the landings and staircases of massive blocks of tenement flats which are slowly replacing the decayed terraces, outside garish pubs and trim betting shops, in the light of coffee bars, cafes and chip saloons, the young people gather at night to follow with almost bored casualness the easy goals of group hedonism.[47]

The terms of the description imply a pessimism about the chances of altering such a culture. It is an attitude that is in odd contradiction with the excited claims made elsewhere in the Report that 'a much larger pool of talent' will be needed in the future. In fact, Newsom declines into bathos with significant regularity: 'The retail trade, for example, is increasingly looking for a better-educated recruit . . . more capable of understanding and reacting effectively to the human situation in which he finds himself.'[48] And the Report's final advocacy of 'an education which is practical, realistic and vocational [which can] make sense to the boys and girls we have in mind'[49] implies little beyond a rather limited kind of schooling.

If Newsom, then, failed to precisely consider manpower needs, it equally did nothing to deliver the curriculum from traditional conceptions of the purposes of mass education. Its overt human concern was accompanied by an endorsement of 'realistic' expectations of occupational destiny, and of the type of education appropriate to it. But it is less the contradictions of Newsom that are important than the types of concern it helped to encourage and the areas that it left neglected.

Reinterpreting equal opportunity

Reports like Newsom did not, of course, lead to sweeping alterations in the curriculum, and the documents of the Schools Council outlined a practice far more progressive than that which was taking place in most schools. Nevertheless, they had the effect of making some issues central and of crowding out others. Research projects, teacher-training courses, curriculum development, all tended to concentrate on issues of removing the 'handicap' which inhibited working-class educational success. The explanatory model of 'handicap' quite swiftly came to be challenged. From the later 1960s the work of some lecturers and of some classroom teachers explored more radical approaches to the problem of 'failure', which stressed the way in which the school inhibited learning, and the way in which the students' own critical consciousness of their environment was a powerful stimulus to learning. There was a willingness, in making this critique, to draw from American and Third World critiques of bureaucratised education, such as those of Kohl and Freire.[50] The context of such developments was, at home, the failure of the Labour Government to take any effective steps to reduce inequality and carry out radical policies, and, internationally, the struggles of the oppressed – whether of Vietnam or of black America – against the world's leading imperialism. Anti-statist, anti-bureaucratic models of education, whether from north-eastern Brazil or the ghettoes of New York, stimulated critiques of the British system. The new interests were expressed with a radical sharpness that had been missing from educational discussion since the 1920s. They are discussed in more detail in Chapter 5.

A consciousness of how ineffective existing policies were even penetrated state-sponsored policy-making, particularly in relation to the problem of the 'inner city'. From 1968 onwards, partly as a response to the speeches of Enoch Powell, which warned of, and promoted, racial conflict in the cities, the Labour Government supported experimental measures of positive discrimination to fund 'urban renewal' and to prevent a collapse of inner-city morale. An important aspect of the project was its emphasis on the role of the communities in such areas in remaking their societies.[51] Equal opportunity was something to be organised, and even fought for, through community pressure, rather than a simple product of an input of government funds and provisions. This, perhaps the most radical point reached by social policy, was the background to the report, *Educational Priority*, prepared for the DES by A. H. Halsey and published in 1972.[52]

Halsey reported on initiatives taken in a number of inner-city areas to raise the level of educational and social achievement, through policies involving much closer links between school and community. His conclusions were radical:

Liberal policies failed, basically, on an inadequate theory of learning. They failed to notice that the major determinants of educational achievement were not schoolmasters but social situations; not curricula, but motivation; nor formal access to the school, but support in families and communities.[53]

Halsey argued for more than the pouring of cash into deprived areas. He envisaged:

a wide range of social reform which would democratise local power structures and diversify local occupational opportunities so that society would look to schools for a supply of young people educated for political and social responsibility and linked to their communities not by failure in the competition but by rich opportunities for work and life.[54]

Halsey supported the Plowden Report's recommendation of Educational Priority Areas (EPAs) as focuses of positive discrimination. Nursery education within these areas was advocated as a crucial means of raising educational standards. The school should be integrated with community and family life. Even with these reforms, the EPAs could only succeed as part of a 'comprehensive social movement towards community development'.

Halsey's suggestions represented the closest relationship yet achieved between measures intended to increase equal opportunity and changes in the curriculum and pedagogy of the school. Indeed, it was plainly stated that the latter were in many ways the necessary conditions for the achievement of the former objective. The report also brought the progressive emphasis on changing relations within the school into its closest contact with an effort to change the conditions outside the school that reproduced disadvantage. The report was the most radically committed document ever produced within an official policy-making framework. Its failure – for it was not seriously taken up – demonstrates some of the weaknesses of the strategies of reform, even at this, one of their highest points.

It was, first, unable to relate its ideas to the material forces that could carry them out. The reforms it proposed were sweeping, yet it sanguinely expected the existing state to implement them – it sought no other support. In fact, the 'Community Development Projects', set up in four urban areas, which had aims closely related to those of Halsey and which had become increasingly critical of local business and political power structures, were closed down during the period in office of the 1974–9 Labour Government. Second, *Educational Priority* continued a tradition of neglecting the effects of the division of labour in society. Halsey tended to separate education from the labour process which was at the root of its systems of selection and discipline. It was one thing to call for 'rich opportunities for work and life' and for an end to the scarring of students by 'failure in competition'. It was quite another to leap from the aim to the means of fighting to realise it. How could rich working opportunities be provided (or local power structures democratised) without an attack on the social relations which underpinned these local forms?

Reform in the classroom

What happened in classroom-orientated work followed a similar path to that of state reform. Newsom had spoken of a cultural alienation among working-class children, an exclusion from what was seen as a (potentially) common national culture. It was especially concerned with problems of communication, speaking of 'boys and girls whose potential is masked by inadequate powers of speech'. Once again, this was an observation that was tinged with anxiety: 'their frustration [may] express itself in apathy or rebelliousness'. 'To arrive at some code of moral and social behaviour which is self-imposed', the experience of students must be lived out in terms of a binding national culture. The desires of Newsom coincided with developing practice in many secondary schools. The popular *English for the Rejected*[55] encouraged work that would relate 'to the large and small crises of everyday life' of 'rejected students' – crises that, by definition, 'have nothing to do with vocation, class, status'. The intention was to approach the 'linguistic handicaps' of students via close attention to their own experience, while at the same time linking this experience to the great emotional universals of the common culture. It was certainly an improvement on endless exercises in the 'skills' of a subject, with little regard to the experience of students. But it continued, though sympathetically, to see students as suffering from cultural handicaps which could be compensated for, not by attention to the causes of deprivation, but by asserting, in the midst of deprivation, a common humanity.

This approach was increasingly superseded by one that not only tried to identify the remediable causes of deprivation, but that questioned the term itself. Writers on language, which had been given the central place in attempts to develop 'working class performance', recognised the way that the nature of the school obstructed the effective use of language by students. Correspondingly, the culture of the home – or, at least, of extra-school activity – was revalued more positively. 'The major educational issue of our time', wrote Douglas Barnes in 1969, 'is our failure to achieve an education which is equally available to members of the various sub-cultures which inhabit our society.'[56] Such an education could be created if teachers stimulated the language activity of their students, and recognised and built on the strengths of the 'various sub-cultures'. By encouraging speech and writing about personal experience, teachers could bring relevance to school activity, achieve the voicing of the experience of particular sub-cultures, and overcome some of the effects of class society. The emphasis was now consciously more pluralist than in the past, no longer concentrating on the inculcation of the values of a 'national' culture.

Ideas like those of Barnes were widespread. Like the ideas of the original progressives, they emphasised the self-activity of the student and the way that the usual operation of the school restricted it. They proposed not just 'good ideas' for the classroom, but a reordering of classroom relations which would allow the free discussion of experience and ideas. In that way, the actions of the students would be profoundly changed. As Barnes put it, 'We educate children in order to change their behaviour by changing their view of the world.'[57]

Barnes's statement raises a problem posed also by progressive ideas of the 1920s. It is clear from Dewey's writing – especially from that on the USSR – that it was from a combination of intellectual *and* practical activity, inside and outside the school, that he intended an understanding of society to arise. It is also plainly the case that Dewey himself retreated from such a position, and that few other progressives conceived of 'activity' as anything other than school-bound activity. (The redefinition of 'activity' to mean 'creative, mental activity' accomplished in the Spens Report is in this sense revealing.) Barnes's work did not escape this problem: education – a process based on primarily linguistic, classroom activity – was intended to alter behaviour by altering world-views. It is arguable that such a project, not linking intellectual to practical activity, was unlikely to succeed as the basis of an effective popular education. It operated, for instance, without reference to post-war changes in the life of the school. For a longer period than before, the student spent the working day in an institution cut off from economic and political activity in a condition of 'infantilisation', deprived of rights and responsibilities. In such a situation, language activity, whatever its benefits, could not fully take the place of responsible practical activity, and certainly could not 'change the students' view of the world'.

A second major pillar of radicalised progressivism was also flawed. 'The curriculum', wrote Halsey, 'should be aimed primarily at the critical and constructive adaptation of children to the actual environment in which they live . . . The balance of the curricular diet should change from academic to social.'[58] Like Barnes, Halsey here tries to theorise a critical and a radical education: one relevant to need. The problem is the restricted focus of relevance. Halsey has justly been criticised for assuming that 'emphasis on reform and change, when founded on local experience, could avoid the risk of diagnosis and prescription *in vacuo* – as if causes and remedies were local, rather than national and international'.[59] Halsey's concerns are those of a radicalised Hadow. The local environment is once more to be brought into the school, this time for critical scrutiny. But both reports reduce education to the local and concrete – neither suggests that education has a general, abstract and intellectual 'moment'.

Nevertheless, positions of this sort, expressed from universities and research projects, encouraged socially committed, even partisan, teaching. Although never the practice of even a large minority of teachers, the combination of progressive method and social radicalism had far more of a purchase on the comprehensive of the 1970s than on the elementary school of the 1920s. It was an influence, though, obtained less by a focused political and intellectual confrontation with existing schooling than by a spontaneous opportunism which rushed into the channels opened by new-found state concerns, and by the ways in which they were interpreted by influential educationalists. As I will show in Chapter 5, the political consequences of this form of advance were unfortunate: an over-estimation of the benevolence of the state, the autonomy of the school and the durability of progressive gains. At the end of the 1960s, for instance, one of the most politically sensitive of progressive educationalists – Doug Holly, in *Society, Schools and Humanity* – could argue that 'it may well be a result of the unique autonomy of British teachers that profound changes can take place here with surprising ease', and anticipate that, once progressive methods had proved themselves, 'Conservative opposition too will then abate and an effective depoliticisation of secondary education will have taken place'.[60]

Progressive continuities

There are continuities between the progressivism of the 1920s and that of post-war decades. The connections are not only those of an intellectual tradition, but arise from the necessarily contradictory outcome of attempts to create, within the state system, models of child-centred education. These attempts have produced both the 'official' progressivism of a Newsom, which shows a concern for the needs of the child within the framework of a conventionally interpreted commitment to the 'needs of society', and also the more radical and dissatisfied positions of a Halsey.

Each era of progressive education displays similar uncertainties and ambiguities, which often concern the relationship between schooling and social destiny and purpose. 'Activity' as a concept aspires to relate education to practical social activity, yet settles for activity within the limits of the classroom. 'Relevance' is sensitive to the experience of the student, yet has not avoided intellectual restrictiveness. Politically, in each era, there has been a quest for state support that has sometimes combined implausibly with sweeping critiques of the ethos of contemporary schooling. The great differences between the different historic forms of progressivism are a result of changes in the role of state education. Sixty years ago, in a system dedicated largely to repression and restricted selection, progressive education had to constitute itself largely outside the state system, exercising only a gradual humanising influence. The attempts in the 1960s to use education as a means to achieve social mobility and class integration gave progressive education a wider scope, a clearer role in social policy and a closer connection with egalitarian ideas. For a short time, the problems encountered by reform were spurs to further radicalisation. That period now is ended. Some of the features of progressive education will continue to survive, whatever the overall nature of the school system, as useful techniques or as islands of radicalism. Its overall concerns, however, no longer find an echo in governments' thinking.

3

The social democratic tradition

There is scarcely any better way for a political party to indicate
its attitude towards the problems of its society's development
today than by the general nature of its education policy.[1]

In 1982 the Labour Party adopted the most radical educational
policy in its history. It included: a statutory right to pre-school
education; the abolition of corporal punishment; the inclusion of
'community co-optees', parents and senior pupils, teaching and
non-teaching staff on the governing bodies of schools; a legal
definition of comprehensive education as 'a system in which all
children have the right to experience a broadly based curriculum,
with equal access to all the opportunities offered in a school'; the
introduction of a common exam for all students at 16 + ; movement
towards the abolition of public schools; a unified and
comprehensive system of 16–19 education.[2]

The first response to these reforms should be supportive – the
second, quizzical. To what extent do they challenge the way in
which education reproduces the different categories of a stratified
labour force? To what extent do they introduce an education
critical of the needs of industry? Do they distinguish between the
simple modernisation of education, and its radical reform?

These churlish questions are occasioned by Labour's educational
record. Over sixty years the Labour Party has indicated its attitude
to the problems of society's development by its failure to
implement – and, mostly, even to suggest – any alternative policies
to those suggested by the course of capitalist progress. This chapter

will consider the educational politics of the Labour Party, and of the trade unions, from the first codifications of a coherent educational policy, in the 1920s, to the onset of crisis in the early 1970s. Chapter 4 discusses Labour's response to that crisis.

Equivocal opportunity

'Equal opportunity' has been the motivating slogan of Labour's programme, without significant challenge, for fifty years. As a precise set of demands, it has gone through many mutations, but its core-meaning remains: equal access for all social classes to education, so as to equalise the occupational chances of the individuals who comprise those classes. Underlying the objective has been an acceptance of the relations of production and inequalities of class which affect these outcomes. The attempt to equalise opportunity, while the structures that promote inequality are left largely untouched, is a less fulfilling task than that of Sisyphus.

These shortcomings of equal opportunity have been pointed out many times.[3] Less frequently observed is their effect on working-class educational politics. 'Equal opportunity' encourages a concern with individual educational outcomes which is divisive in two ways. It not only discourages any attempt to define educational purpose in terms of the advancement of the class as a whole, but also fosters a positive hostility between individual educational betterment and collective advance; it offers, as one of its beneficiaries caustically put it, equality of opportunity to escape from working-class life.[4] Earlier socialist educational traditions were aware of this danger. One trade-union pamphlet, in 1909, warned that the government would select boys from elementary schools and offer them a schooling based on 'a sociology in which the individual is understood to be dependent on his *own* thrift, his *own* interest for his *own* success in life – a sociology under which property is sacred'. The class system would perpetuate itself, by taking working-class children 'because they were intelligent and dangerous, away from their class'.[5] But more typical, even at this time, was the perspective outlined by the Labour Party in 1906, of putting secondary education 'within the reach of every child whose *usefulness* would be enhanced by such extended education'.[6]

Equal opportunity can carry a stronger interpretation: a commitment to positive discrimination, or to the eradication of educational privilege. But these aspects have not been dominant. The perspective has been one of advancing working-class interests without challenging the existing distribution of knowledge and power.

Defeating a rival

Equal opportunity is conventionally presented as *the* expression of working-class educational aims, as if it summed up the wisdom and experience of the class. In fact, like most other political ideologies, it achieved its dominance only after successfully contesting other objectives and strategies. It became the decisive – almost the sole – influence on Labour Party policy in the 1920s. Before then, it had existed alongside a belief that working-class educational objectives should be fundamentally different from those of other classes, directed towards forming consciousness of the need for socialism. Therefore, although equal access to education was not ignored, there was, in this belief, an insistence on the importance of educational content, and on popular control of the education system. The early 1920s saw a battle in the main organisations of the working class between this outlook and one that emphasised above all the need to widen access to the system, for reasons of social justice, harmony, and economic efficiency.

The more critical tendency was based not so much on the Labour Party as on the industrial trade unions. It saw education as a weapon of political struggle, a means of developing socialist consciousness. Movements of adult self-education, such as the Plebs League, offered a counter-education based on Marxist philosophy and economics. Although confined to a few areas, such as South Wales, its influence alarmed the Commissioners asked by Lloyd George in 1917 to investigate industrial unrest. By 1926, over 30,000 adults were enrolled in Plebs or similar classes,[7] which had substantial support from the rail and mining unions. Although always a minority, the movement influenced the TUC to accept, in the mid-1920s, that Marxism should be part of the syllabus of the proposed TUC education centre.[8] Similarly, its educational aims influenced debate at Labour Party and trade-union conferences, and also led in some areas to direct contestation of the most overtly conservative aspects of state education, such as Empire Day. Beyond such specific struggles, though, it had little practical concern with schooling. This had nothing to do with a view of state education as neutral. It was more that the state system was regarded as too powerful and reactionary a force to allow any scope for struggle within it. Efforts were devoted more to establishing a counter-system than with making demands on the state.

These ideas were anathema to the Labour Party's Advisory Committee on Education. Founded at the beginning of the 1920s to elaborate a detailed Labour policy, this was a non-elected body consisting of experts from academic and progressive educational life. It had, and sought, few links with the trade unions, though they later turned to it as a source of policy. Over a decade, the ACE developed detailed educational proposals, based on increasing access to the state system: plans that could be carried out either by a future Labour Government or through pressure on the existing system (several of the ACE's members sat on the Consultative Committees of the Board of Education). There was certainly no thought of direct political action to implement its proposals.

The ACE's programme rested on Labour's philosophy of education. For Ramsay MacDonald, 'Labour strove to transform education, through raising the standards of mental and moral qualities, through the acceptance of programmes by reason of their justice, rationality and wisdom.'[9] This conception in no way counterposed 'socialist' to 'bourgeois' ideas. Education was a single, beneficent whole. 'You gave us', one Labour MP told the House of Commons in 1922, 'an Education Act 46 or 47 years ago and, such as it was, it gave us knowledge, and knowledge is power.'[10] 'Education' and 'knowledge' thus had no precise meaning – but were constantly associated with the higher things in life. 'Socialists know that good education is the key to another world', wrote the Independent Labour Party (ILP) in 1923.[11] It was the ACE, and R. H. Tawney in particular, who translated the notion of 'education-as-such' being a good thing into a concern for concrete and gradualist reform of the education system, so as to purge it of class bias and make its undoubted benefits more widely available. In the process, the ACE drew up a particular, limited definition of equal opportunity, and, simultaneously, prepared schemes for the transformation of working-class life through education. In this latter light, nursery education was recommended, as a means of compensating for the worst features of working-class life. A nursery system could:

> send a million children on – clean, intelligent, accustomed to work in a garden, to read and spell well, to write, [to be] sound, as far as it goes, in dealing with number, accustomed to wear nice clothes, to eat and behave politely, well-nourished and free of ailments.[12]

The ACE's major production, Tawney's *Secondary Education For All*, likewise took its distance from questions of class interest: 'Labour's policy is not for the advantage of any single class, but to develop the human resources of the whole community.'[13] Tawney's proposals fell well short of comprehensive education; the development of the human resources of the community required selective secondary education.

But less important than the precise nature of reform was the subordination of working-class educational interests to those of long-term state policy. Tawney's counter-position of class to community was made, not to demonstrate to working-class organisations that they had to develop policies that would allow them to win hegemony over intermediate social layers, but to encourage them to renounce the attempt to formulate their own independent politics and instead seek influence upon state policy-making. Built into the project was a remoteness of educational policy from working-class activity, and an accompanying dismissal of the Plebs' slogan: 'for an independent working-class education'. With the codification of Labour's programme, as a prelude to government, it became necessary for the supporters of the ACE's line to fix Labour's course permanently, through inflicting a conclusive defeat on ideas that had previously co-existed with those of the equal opportunity programme.

The battle between the ACE and the class-conscious ideologies was fought out in the mid-1920s, and ended in the defeat of the left. The main cause of defeat lay outside education, in the fate of the General Strike, and the drastic weakening of the Miners' Federation, the main base of independent educational movements. The lost battle of 1926 gave impetus to right-wing trends in the labour movement and strengthened the central bureaucracies of the Labour Party and the unions – who proceeded to a thorough witch-hunt of their decimated opponents. The tactics of the ACE in this operation were to avoid open confrontation with its opponents and instead to rely on silence, evasion, manipulation of debate. When the Labour Conference of 1926, for instance, called for a 'workers' committee of inquiry' into education, to determine how it might serve working-class purposes, the Labour leadership was quick to decide that the ACE itself constituted such a committee. The ACE reported:

> We should regard as . . . reactionary and contrary to the best traditions of public education in this country an attempt to impose on immature young minds a particular labour or socialist creed, or any brand of class-conscious psychology . . . It is . . . not the function of the school to play a direct part in abolishing the present or creating a new order of society, but we rely on the strengthening of character and the growth of intelligence which are the fruits of true education to prepare the way for the realisation of labour and socialist ideals.[14]

As it happened, this report was neither delivered nor published, and debate was avoided. Instead, more administrative methods were used to settle differences. In January 1927, Labour MPs and members of the ACE split the militant Labour teachers' organisation, the Teachers' Labour League (TLL), in protest against its 'anti-religious and class-conscious teachings'.[15] In the following summer holidays – always a good time for bureaucratic manoeuvre – the TLL was summarily expelled, without hearing or investigation, from the Labour Party on the grounds that it had fallen under Communist influence. At the same time, the TUC General Council felt able to drop Marxism from its proposed courses of trade-union education, which became merely a form of vocational training for trade-union officials.[16]

These defeats had lasting consequences: the near obliteration of radical-socialist movements, critical of the existing system, and with a substantial working-class base. But it would be sentimental to attribute such near-total eclipse simply to the effectiveness of persecution. It was also the case that the left was incapable of coming to terms with what was new in education. The right was able to point to the changes taking place within state education which made it less authoritarian and which broadened access. It could argue that the future was one of the continued expansion and modernisation of education, and that the policies of the ACE would then come into their own, since no other party was so clear about its educational goals, nor so in touch with the progressive movements that were changing education. It could claim that the left neglected the developments that were taking place, ignored the necessity of Labour appealing to sectors of the population outside the heavy-industrial working class, and merely restated timeless dogmas.

A clash between the two positions occurred at the 1927 TUC. The General Council reported the evidence it had submitted, after consulting the ACE, to a Government Committee. This was a statement of welcome for progressive methods, which, it said, had caused standards to rise, and created a more relevant, less punitive kind of education. The TUC evidence had tried to strengthen a particular trend within state education, not to condemn the whole system; the strategy was that of a pressure group, rather than of a campaigning movement.

From the floor, Miss M. Birch of the Workers' Union attacked the evidence. It put up no 'real opposition against the anti-working class education which is dispensed from elementary schools to children of the working class'. Specifically, 'no attempt is made to show that history should be the history of the development of society determined by the manner in which the means of production are owned and controlled'.[17] In support, another speaker claimed that if textbooks were based on the materialist conception of history 'we would have an entirely different outlook'. The scope and acuity of the critique did not match its vigour. It dealt only with one peripheral subject that was the most amenable to discussion in political terms, and neglected wider questions of curriculum and method. Nothing was said about the new education for which the Council sought the approval of Congress. To this extent, the left did not enter the debate. It appeared to be archaic in its arguments and outlandish in its strategy. J. W. Bowen, replying for the General Council, described the critique as 'stock phraseology' – as indeed it was, the points having first been made in the 1880s. 'We could not go to an impartial tribunal', said Bowen, 'and urge upon them the class warfare.' Besides, 'History is not the only subject . . . After all said and done, you cannot very well relate the class warfare to a problem in geometry.'[18]

It would be comforting to see Bowen's reply (he won the debate) as simply a bureaucratic brush-off. He identified a real weakness behind the bravura declarations of class hostility in the left's arguments: it had very little to say about the exact relationship between education and the political and economic order. At a time when economic need was very slowly beginning to exert different pressures on education and when the political requirements made of it were no longer simply those of fervent nationalism and rigid discipline, it was no longer adequate to reiterate old certainties about the way that education functioned. Some modernisation of socialist educational attitudes was necessary if left-wing critiques were not to lose their efficacy. This did not occur, a failure that sounded the death knell of the independent working-class educational tradition as a significant political force.

Consolidation

The left, then, faced two kinds of problem. The first – the increased power that the defeat of the General Strike had given its opponents – it could do little about. But this situation also produced a set of strategies specifically intended as an alternative to the path of militant working-class struggle, which, according to the TUC, was 'futile, certain to fail, and sure to lead to bloodshed and misery'.[19] In industry, this strategy produced 'Mondism', a policy of collaboration between the unions and advanced industrialists in pursuit of economic growth and social reform. In education, it meant backing for the ACE and the search for allies among administrators and industrialists who would join a campaign in support of limited educational reform. This programme did not include, for instance, multilateral education, curtailment of church schools, or any measures directed against the public schools. In the late 1920s, the left was no longer strong enough to put forward a realistic alternative programme of action. The tasks it faced were twofold; it had to modernise its educational policies, without collapsing them into those of the ACE, and it had to aim at converting itself into the militant left wing of the reforming movement, pushing for the most radical interpretation of equal opportunity. It had the problem of criticising the premises and content of Labour's new strategy, in such a way that reforms could be supported without the objectives of a Tawney coming to represent the farthest limit of working-class educational perspectives. In this respect, the story is one of failure.

In the absence of any alternative, the Labour Party – leadership and rank-and-file – swung towards acceptance of progressive education. Both were attracted by the way progressivism broadened and humanised ideas of education. Delegations from the educationally influential Bradford ILP, for instance, which visited progressive state schools in England and in socialist Vienna, were entranced by the scope allowed to the activity of children, the affability of the teachers, and even the colours of the innovatory wall-charts.[20] Progressive methods had a human appeal which the advocates of class-conscious education found difficult to match. A Labour pamphlet of 1930 had as its epigraph a quotation from the Hadow Report, 'The aim of education is to provide an environment so that each individual develops to the fullest possible extent his innate power',[21] and it was surely the stress of individual development that attracted, rather than the more subdued qualification, 'fullest possible extent', with its suggestion of different levels of attainment and outcome.

If the defeat of the left in the working-class movement was one reason for the rise of equal opportunity, another was its appropriateness as a means of satisfying economic and political need. At the same time as education felt the push of progressivism, it was also pulled into new shapes by economic compulsion – the need for great numbers of technicians and white-collar workers. Even by the early 1920s a third of secondary places, in response to this need, were free, not bought, and the increasing rate of transfer to secondary schools meant that elementaries had to provide at least a basis for secondary work.

Such developments seem to represent the natural course of educational evolution. But between the wars they faced the obdurate opposition of many sections of the ruling class and middle class. Farmers and textile manufacturers opposed the raising of the leaving age to 15. The Anglican Church controlled a huge, impoverished and backward sector of the elementary schools. Working-class Catholics in the Labour Party prevented a

Labour Government raising the leaving-age until they had secured the right to control their own schools. Early monetarists destroyed the plans for expansion laid by the Education Act of 1918. Conservative obscurantism, at all levels of the party, retarded the mildest modernisation. Lord Irwin, President of the Board of Education in 1924, was not a notable reformer: 'We need a new church school here', he said on a visit to his family estate. 'Will the Board agree? We want a school to train them up for servants and butlers.'[22] Such backwardness, verging on stupidity, had important results. It forced an alliance between Labour and the trade unions, teachers, local education authorities and more enlightened capitalists such as Woolton, a shopping magnate and later Conservative Minister, and Nuffield of Morris Motors. All were in favour of educational growth and modernisation. In the context of the reforming alliance, modernisation was linked to social reform and equal opportunity. Although, from a left-wing point of view, the ACE's ideas had collapsed socialist educational perspectives into the fight for a limited programme of reform, it was also the case that the hopelessly reactionary nature of government policy handed strategic initiative to the Labour Party. The reform of English education was thus perceived via the problem of equal opportunity, and the development of a clear-sighted educational policy hindered, The questions of access and of economic efficiency seemed to be two sides of the same coin: they were not.

By the mid-1930s, a lasting pattern of educational politics had been set. The radical working-class tradition had itself been uprooted. Teacher militancy was non-existent. Governments were lobbied by wide coalitions of educational interests. The most abrasive educational conservatisms were being weakened: many authorities no longer celebrated Empire Day. The government and the more backward sections of the ruling class apart, consensus surrounded the definition of objectives. The Spens Report, in 1938, recommended secondary education for all. At the same time, the TUC put forward a similar view, in revealing terms. It described the elementary/secondary divide as 'the last great class barrier' in education.[23] Considering that the public schools were still thriving, and that there were no official proposals for abolishing selection at the age of 11, the TUC's statement was modest indeed.

Despite the developing consensus, the educational policies of the governments of the 1930s were virtually immobile. Expenditure on elementary schools, for instance, was scarcely higher in 1937 than in 1921. The number of elementary teachers was no greater.[24] Given the consensus over educational aims, the battles now centred on the government's unwillingness to finance provision. As Brian Simon puts it, 'the inter-war years were dominated by the cry for economy'.[25]

The extremes of class privilege were blatant. Only 1 per cent of students at Oxford and Cambridge, for instance, were of working-class origin;[26] two and a quarter million children were taught in classes larger than forty; 5 per cent of all children were officially classified as under-nourished.[27] In this situation, anger, outrage and the cry for reform were justifiable enough. The problem was that this was the point at which labour movement policies halted.

The weakness of 1944

The first major achievement of the reforming movement – the 1944 Education Act – shows this clearly enough. In the war years, all political parties finally accepted that neither the political nor the economic situation allowed a continuation of the old order. Even Churchill, not the most active of reformers, recognised this. He wrote in 1944, 'I do not think we can maintain our position in the post-war world unless we are an exceptionally well-educated people.'[28] In the same year, the Government's McNair Committee discovered that only 21,000 students stayed on at school after their seventeenth birthday, yet they were 'the main source of supply for the professions . . . scientists, higher technicians and administrators'.[29]

It could, of course, be pointed out that similar sentiments were widespread at the end of the First World War, yet did not prevent the non-implementation of important parts of the 1918 Education Act. This time, however, the pressures for change – in the form of the labour and trade-union movement – were very much stronger. R. A. Butler, architect of the 1944 Act, anticipated that this strength would create major problems over the future of the public schools and of the church sector.

As it turned out, his worries were misplaced. The organisational strength of the labour movement was not matched by a radical political force. Butler's reforms raised the school-leaving age to 15, in effect replaced the elementary school by the secondary modern and offered free state secondary education to all. Butler provided continued support for church schools, so long as they submitted to supervision, strengthened direct-grant grammar schools and did not threaten public school education. Yet the labour movement, content that a large part of its programme was about to be realised, did not consider the Act as a contribution to the maintenance of class inequality. Conservatives were reassured that it did not threaten privilege, religion or selective hierarchies. *The Times* could comment on the Commons debate on the Act: 'Not a single voice was raised in favour of holding up or whittling down any one of the proposals for educational advance embodied in the White Paper.'[30]

The 1944 settlement left standing many of the pillars of the system. Even so, it aroused little controversy. Only six MPs (a minority of them from the Labour Party) voted to abolish public schools. The tripartite system was accepted and defended by Ellen Wilkinson, former member of the Plebs League and Labour's first post-war Minister of Education.[31]

The Act was welcomed by the Labour Party as a giant progressive step. Communist militants argued that its reforms were so sweeping that they left behind only pockets of ruling-class resistance that could later be mopped up. Both assessments were wrong. The reforms did not open the way to fundamental change. They were introduced so that, as far as possible, things could remain the same. As Quintin Hogg realised, they succeeded, for twenty-five years, in placing 'the general framework of our educational system beyond party politics'.[32] Education was now in the same category of things-not-to-be-questioned as the British constitution. The contrast with the early 1920s could not have been more acute.

But this political achievement did not mean that education was now efficiently integrated into national economic planning. Butler had identified three major problems and solved two of them – the church and public schools. The third – the linking of the schools with employment needs – was less tractable. Little was said about the kind of education that should occur in the new system. The *TES*, in May 1945, wrote that:

The central educational problem of today is to create a modern synthesis, a common core of studies and activities as integrative of culture as has been for centuries the study of the languages, the literature and the thought of Greece and Rome.

But it cannot be said that this task was seriously undertaken. The academic traditions of the grammar school were unaltered. Technical schools were so underdeveloped that they never amounted to more than 5 per cent of secondary-school numbers. Secondary moderns were seen as the home of 'concrete' and restricted, rather than generally formative, activities. No plan existed to make use of their resources. Quite the opposite: secondary moderns were discouraged from entering their students for the public examinations that could qualify them for non-manual jobs. In response to the requirements of the job market they entered, students did so unofficially.

Withering roots

Whatever the weaknesses of the policies they supported, the campaigns that led up to the 1944 Act had some of the qualities of a movement: some degree of popular support and involvement.[33] Their goals expressed the desire of working-class organisations for collective educational advance. Even though self-education movements were in decline, there remained a vague commitment to the intrinsic value of education. 'Love learning which is the food of the mind, and be grateful to your teachers as your parents', as one of the commandments of the Socialist Sunday Schools had once put it.[34] Universal, free state education, in the form provided by the Act, weakened such impulses. The commitment to 'learning' could not be easily sustained if the organisation of learning was to be the responsibility of a state system based firmly on the allocation of individuals to particular places in the division of labour. Not only would the original impulse of reform then atrophy, but the very commitment to learning diminish, as it became bound up either with escape from working-class life, or associated with the daily petty repressions of schooling. So the apparent realisation of long-sought goals increased, in fact, the speed of decay of the aspirations that had originally nourished them. The 1944 Act offered nothing in the way of popular involvement in education that would have counteracted this tendency.

Some such development would probably have been a side-effect of any increase in state intervention, especially after the interwar defeats and the breaking up of the communities and organisations that had sustained militant activity. But it was accelerated and sharpened by the activities of the Labour Party. The Party's developing commitment to comprehensive education in the 1950s should not be taken as an index of growing radicalism. Its presentation of equal opportunity put more stress on the attractive individual destinies it could offer, and even less on its function as a means of collective advance. Labour supported comprehensives partly on grounds of economic efficiency and partly on those of social justice. This was no different from the way it had previously supported secondary education for all. But there was a substantial difference between this and the earlier campaign. The pre-war separation of state education into elementary and secondary sectors was a form of discrimination whose class basis was clear to all who criticised it. Its replacement by what was apparently a system of selection by ability seemed to displace the issue of failure from a class to an individual level. The 'eleven-plus' took into each family (or at least into those motivated towards educational success) the traumas of success or failure at school. Family and school rituals grew up around the examination. Eleven-plus streams (and therefore non-exam streams) were established in primary schools. Mock-tests in Arithmetic, English and 'Aptitude' were held for months beforehand; sheaves of testing books were bought privately by parents. Schools excluded on the day of exams all those who were not taking them. Later came the head-teacher's formal entry to the classroom to begin the ceremony of results; the shedding of tears and the offering of consolation; the immediate release for the day of those who passed; the rewards and presents for success.[35] Press coverage partly reflected, partly stimulated these hopes and fears. 'Is your child doomed at a Modern School?' 'Is it failure to send John to a new-type Modern School?' 'Would you call this a second-best school?'[36]

It was to these concerns that Labour's electoral propaganda was orientated; some material even dramatised the family predicament in cartoon form. The nub of its policy was less the planned development of comprehensive education than the abolition of the eleven-plus. It said little about the internal organisation or curriculum of the new school. No government reports preceded the issue of Circular 10/65 which encouraged local authorities to end selection. A House of Commons motion passed at the time simply said that comprehensives would 'preserve all that is valuable in grammar school education . . . and make it more widely available to more children'.[37]

Attention to parental aspirations was complemented by Harold Wilson's ability to connect comprehensive reform with the needs of industrial modernisation. His rhetoric of 'technological revolution' was a successful popularisation of what both major parties saw as a necessary modernisation of industry, in which state intervention would play a considerable part, and which would entail expansion and reshaping of the social infrastructure of the country, especially the schools and universities, intended to be egalitarian powerhouses of economic renewal.

As an electoral strategy, modernised grammar-school education for all was a great success – it was the second most popular issue among Labour voters at the 1964 election,[38] and an important asset in Labour's efforts to win the electoral support of the 'middle layers' in society. But in promoting the issue in the way that it did, Labour was further weakening conceptions of education as a means of collective advancement. The stress was placed, rather, on the benefits it awarded the individual. There is nothing, of course, automatically reactionary about parental interest in schooling; but Labour, in linking it to educational objectives that were mostly related to the school's success in preparing children for the labour market, implied that the measure of the school's worth lay in the number of qualifications it could provide. Two decades later, the Conservatives were to encourage parents to be the vigilantes of education, ferocious in defence of kin, single-minded in pursuit of narrow objectives. The pre-existing attitudes to which they could appeal were partly a result of the way Labour shaped parental aspirations in its comprehensive campaign.

Labour raised expectations of the comprehensive higher than its politics could deliver. In the 1950s, problems of failure and indiscipline could be explained as the consequence of a divided system. A mid-decade panic over 'blackboard jungles' was related to such a diagnosis. Comprehensives, it was argued, could solve the problems that arose from frustration and lack of opportunity. This unconvincing promise was related to Labour's failure to grasp the (capitalist) economic requirements pointed to by the Crowther Report. In Crowther's view, there were two different kinds of 'need'. The first was for a small, though growing, layer of specialists, professionals and technicians; the second, for a much less well qualified work-force. The latter group required, nevertheless, some 'general mechanical intelligence' and sense of civic responsibility. Labour tended to neglect the difference between the two types of need; its rhetoric of opportunity suggested that, by following and reflecting trends in the economy, the school could open up new areas of opportunity and deliver to all a more fulfilling education. It was not a claim that stood the test of events. Labour also ignored the effect of schooling on its clientele. It presented the school as an unequivocal benefit. It neglected the low-level education to which the demand for general mechanical intelligence gave rise. It was not a party that championed discontent with the education system. Quite the opposite, in fact. Labour was extremely hesitant in acting against local authorities which obstructed comprehensive reform, and utterly paralysed in its dealings with public schools. Conversely, its post-war record in dealing with radical opposition to aspects of state schooling is a robustly reactionary one. Labour ministers in the late 1940s warned against the 'spreading influence' of Communism in schools.[39] Edward Short, Secretary of State for Education in 1968, was quick when faced with student rebellion to characterise the rebels as 'academic thugs'. His response to the strikes of teachers in the following year was to urge them to preserve the professional attitudes of their past.[40] The Labour-controlled ILEA can hardly have been said to have used anything but administrative and punitive measures to deal with the educational problems posed at William Tyndale Junior School in 1975–6.[41]

These, of course, were only the spectacular tips of Labour's bureaucratic and oppressive aspect. Routines of nepotism determined teacher employment in South Wales and the English North East. Labour councils have proved assiduous opponents of teacher trade unionism and parental campaigns against school closure.[42] At no time, in national office, did Labour encourage any popular involvement in the discussion and implementation of educational aims.

Yet Labour, in power or opposition, has faced educational

radicalism only at the periphery of the system. It has never had to withstand a challenge, within the party or the affiliated unions, to the central features of its educational policies. Least of all has it encountered from these quarters opposition to the unproblematic connection it claims between educational reform and economic growth, and to the upholding of a supposed educational neutrality which has been its hallmark since the days of the ACE. It is from the questioning of these principles that present opposition to Labour's policies must begin.

4

The crisis in education

The major change of the last decade has been the eviction of 'equal opportunity' from its place as the central reference point of educational strategy. It is this process that allows us to speak of 'crisis'. For state education policy, the crisis is a time for restructuring and adaptation: it is not a crisis of survival. For the forces that have, traditionally and most firmly, adhered to the policy of equal opportunity, and associated curricular reforms, it is a crisis of a more serious kind, which contains elements of setback and defeat.

Equal opportunity evicted

Proposals to extend equal opportunity did not, of course, disappear in the 1970s. Its extension to women and ethnic minorities was a minor theme of the 'Great Debate'. It still retained a grip on the labour movement, and continued to make some, slowed progress in schools, with a partial abolition of streaming in hundreds of comprehensives. But as the basis and organising principle of educational discussion, state research and policy initiative, and school-based innovation, equal opportunity has lost its role. Inspectorate advice has discouraged the further extension of unstreamed teaching, and promoted, alongside streaming, vocational and work-orientated courses. Research projects and spending initiatives have aimed to monitor 'standards' and encourage expansion only where it helped cope with youth unemployment and provide non-advanced forms of training. Examination policy lessened the influence of teachers and their organisations and, by preserving many features of the two-tier 16 + examination system, prevented the spread of unstreamed teaching to the fourth and fifth years of the secondary school. And, of course, there have been the cuts. Talk of equal opportunity and a 'broad' education has become infrequent.

The displacement of equal opportunity has been the result of two developments: one, a realisation by policy-makers that there was no necessary connection between a widening of access to education and economic efficiency; the other, a resurgence of right-wing educational ideologies and given partial expression in Conservative Party policy. The overall context of these developments has been the renaissance, in a period of economic recession and industrial decline, of free market economics and *laissez-faire* social philosophy which has sought to reduce public spending and state intervention in some fields, while strengthening the authority of the state in others, notably those concerned with law and order.[1] These developments have ensured that equal opportunity has lost much of its influence on policy-making, as well as its ability to form the terms and horizons of popular educational debate.

The most visible effect of this combination of policies has been the withholding of funds from public education. The cuts in educational, especially capital, spending which began in earnest in 1975 imposed limits on expansion and thus on the further growth of measures intended to promote equal opportunity. The cuts especially affected areas important to the positive discrimination recommended as a means of ending 'disadvantage'. The modest aim of the Plowden Report in 1967 was to provide nursery places for 90 per cent of 4-year-olds and 50 per cent of 3-year-olds. The cuts made these targets implausible. 'The achievement of conferring money', confessed Shirley Williams in 1979, 'for half the nursery age group is still far short of our Plowden targets.' Yet it was this area – pre-schooling – that Halsey regarded as 'the outstanding and most effective device in any general approach to raising the educational achievement of working-class children'.[2]

Similar cuts in school meals, adult education and university places widened educational inequalities. The proportion of children of manual workers among university students actually fell from 26 per cent to 23 per cent in 1978.[3] Fringe areas of the curriculum, notably remedial reading classes, began to disappear. An increase in the rate of school closures affected those areas most which, in addition to a 'natural' fall in the birth-rate, were unattractive to capital investment. In these areas – the inner cities, the rural shires – a flight of capital led to a loss of population, low wage levels and an aggravation of crisis. School closures, concentrated in such areas, doubly and trebly penalised them for their unattractiveness to capital.

Such cuts, begun by Labour well before 1979, continued with enthusiasm by the Conservatives, were qualitative in their effect. The secular tendency had been for schools to incorporate into their educational role a welfare function. One of the earliest fights of the TUC had been the eventually successful campaign for midday maintenance: school meals. Likewise, nursery provision was not simply intended to be of educational benefit; it was also a partial transfer of welfare responsibility from the home to the school, made necessary by the increasing employment of women outside the home. To cut such provision was therefore not only to deprive the overwhelmingly female workforce of jobs, and children of care and education, but also to renew some old burdens and reverse an historic trend.

School, work and unemployment: Labour's contribution, 1976–9

But the limits on educational growth were not only made up of cash restrictions. Mass youth unemployment and the great decrease in skilled and long-term job opportunities challenged the assumptions that 'the world of work' required of schools the production of an ever-more-skilled workforce. Instead, it was more openly declared that in the face of competition from other nations a major restructuring and shakeout would occur in British industry. The main qualities this would require from the workforce were those of 'tolerance' and 'adaptability', rather than advanced knowledge of the new technology. The educational strategies of the later 1970s thus placed greater stress on education's *ideological* role in relation to economic development; the relationship of schools to industry was not presented in purely technical terms. They should not be the mere inculcators of vocational skills but, consciously, the presenters of a particular world-view. The Labour Government's 1977 Green Paper made this clear:

Underlying all this [criticism] was the feeling that the educational system was out of touch with the fundamental need for Britain to survive economically in a highly competitive world through the efficiency of its industry and commerce. Some of these criticisms are fair. There is a wide gap between the world of education and the world of work. Boys and girls are not sufficiently aware of the importance of industry to our society, and they are not taught much about it . . . The country's economic well-being depends on its own efforts, and its standard of living is directly related to its ability to sell goods and services overseas . . . We depend upon industry to create the wealth without which our social services, our education and arts cannot flourish.[4]

In this way, the Green Paper encouraged an education of the entire workforce – not simply the future industrial workers – in the importance of working for the nation.

What led a Labour Government to define so implacably the utilitarian goals of education? First, the Green Paper was entirely compatible with Labour's economic policy. As Denis Healey stated: 'It is because our manufacturing industry has declined since the war both in size and efficiency by comparison with those of our competitors that our economic record since the war has been inferior to theirs.' The remedy required 'a major shift in the use of our resources away from private and public consumption towards export and investment'.[5] This policy suggested not only education cuts, but the changes in the character of education proposed by the Green Paper.

Second, it was a product, not just of the priorities of government, but of the state administration. In 1976, a confidential memorandum to the Prime Minister from the Inspectorate had argued:

Some teachers and some schools may have over-emphasised the importance of preparing boys and girls for their role in society compared with the need to prepare them for their economic role . . . Here the time may now be ripe for a change (as the national mood and government policies have changed in the face of hard and irreducible economic facts).[6]

A rethinking of policy

The call for change implied a self-criticism. It was impelled by the chastening review of DES policy-making carried out in 1975 by the Organisation for Economic Co-operation and Development. The OECD had criticised the acceptance by successive governments, without question or discussion, of the prevailing educational wisdom. The criticism reinforced the casual revelations of former ministers. Sir David Eccles had mentioned that, in his five years at Education, the cabinet had only discussed matters educational on one occasion – when the proposed Oxford Ring Road threatened University life and recreation. Edward Boyle, likewise, had explained his encouragement of educational reform, not by reference to government policy decisions, but by saying that 'change was in the air' at the time.[7]

The OECD report was based on much discussion with civil servants, and on a close and critical interrogation of the assumptions of the 1972 White Paper *A Framework for Expansion*. This (Conservative) paper had announced the continuation of the policies of the 1960s, in the guise of perspectives for the next decade:

> The last ten years have seen a major expansion of the education service. The next ten will see expansion continue . . . It is on matters of scale, organisation and cost, rather than educational content that attention is mainly focused in this White Paper.[8]

The OECD noted an absence here of interest in social, economic and technological change, and a lack of critical self-awareness. Its own opinion of current trends was that:

> The British economy has lagged in its development. To the extent that this is due to educational inadequacies, for example in the recruiting and training of workers and managers at the levels of skill [required], large changes of a fundamental, structural

kind will be needed. The question they raise is whether planning that is essentially acquiescent in relation to the dominant opinion is sufficient.[9]

Here it was scathing about the vagueness of the DES's goals 'to develop powers of reasoning and the capacity to adapt to changing circumstances . . . to provide systematic guidance and help so as to develop the power of making informed choices'. 'How', asked the OECD of such definite echoes of progressivism, 'can such objectives be achieved without reference to, or outside the context of, industrial and vocational training?'[10]

Labour and the Right

It is clear that the Green Paper, and the policy initiatives that followed it, were a response to such criticisms. However, Labour's educational policy was not simply a reflex of industrial need and civil service prodding. It was also a calculated response to right-wing criticisms of education, and thus, also a measure of their effectiveness. Labour's Green Paper was more than a codification of a change of perspective by the educational administration. It was part of Labour's 'Great Debate', itself a political reaction to the break-up of the consensus of aims which had existed in the initial years of Labour reform. Labour's response to the right wing was less repudiation than incorporation. In the speech that inaugurated the 'Great Debate', James Callaghan reiterated the criticisms of the right:

> I am concerned on my journeys to find complaints from industry that new recruits from the schools do not have the basic tools to do the job that is required . . . There is unease felt about the new informal methods which seem to produce excellent results when they are in well-qualified hands, but are much more dubious in their effects when they are not.[11]

Thus Callaghan, in probably the most publicised Prime Ministerial speech on education this century, adopted a method that was already familiar to opponents of progressive education. He utilised the difficulties of its implementation, not as a spur to further experiment and effort, but as reasons for changing the emphasis of curricular policy quite markedly. He here might have talked about the great obstacles that impeded equal opportunity and the deep social roots of such obstructions. Instead, noting that for many of the original supporters of reform schooling had not been the promised key to social problems, he linked this perception, and the insecurity that accompanied it, to the DES and CBI critique of education. Rather than working to extend equality of opportunity, he suggested that the eventual laying-to-rest of popular fears was somehow connected to the strengthening of the links between the school and industry. By making the 'world of work' the figurehead of policy, he implied that Labour's traditional conceptions of educational advance were now less important.

Right and Left compared: class contestation

Callaghan's change of direction revealed more than the traditional opportunism of a Labour leader. The unchallenged ease with which it was accomplished was an indication of the weakness of the policy of the labour movement as a whole. Moreover, the targets of his criticism were not those traditionally identified by his party. Rather than attacking the persistence of the old, Callaghan chose to highlight the problems of the (relatively) new reforms associated with progressivism. In doing so, he was recognising the forcefulness of a rejuvenated right-wing critique of state education.

The years 1968–9 were the time of the 'student revolt', whose ripples spread in the next decade through the state institutions. They were also the years of the rebirth of the organised educational right wing, in the form of the Black Papers on education.[12] It is instructive to compare these two challenges to educational orthodoxy. That of the left was based on trade-union militancy, and on a *practical* critique of the curriculum. The two largest teaching unions affiliated to the TUC, and went on strike in 1969 and again, in London, in 1974 over pay. A minority sought to turn the curriculum in a radical direction, emphasising especially anti-racism and anti-sexism. The operation of schools in their regular patterns of selection, moralising and repression was questioned. Radical demands no longer related simply to the expansion of education, but questioned its content and procedures. At the same time came the first organised school-student militancy since the 1920s. In the early 1970s, there were a number of student strikes against the dismissal of popular teachers, and against the infantilisation to which students were subject: in particular, school uniform and corporal punishment. Likewise, from the women's movement and from black communities, criticism of schooling grew. Black parents, for instance, denounced the racist criteria applied in the labelling of their children as subnormal.[13]

But the radicalism associated with 1968 occurred outside the traditional organisations of the labour movement and did not confront its central ideologies. It stressed the class character of the state institutions: they were there to defend and reproduce the existing order. 'Equal opportunity' was inadequate because it failed to understand this function. This point having been made, the debate was not continued; there was no practical, organised attempt to replace the traditional ideology. In addition, although the new radicalism was alert to the authoritarian ideologies generated by the school system, it was largely unconcerned with the relation of education to production. This, too, hindered it from responding to the crisis in traditional reforming strategies. In this respect it was very much a child of the long post-war boom; it scarcely anticipated the changes that recession and economic restructuring would demand of education.

Observers on the right could have dismissed these developments, on their own, as signs only of marginal tension. More worrying was the evidence that the dominant educational ideologies were themselves soft on their left flank: they seemed unconcerned with industrial need, incapable of reproducing ideologies that validated existing interests, and all too willing to give scope to further investigation of the roots of inequalities. Equal opportunity seemed to have become an offensive slogan, intent not on spreading the benefits of the grammar school more widely, but of ending the grammar-school model altogether. Labour's proposals to act against grammar and public schools were hardly a comprehensive socialist programme, but were nevertheless enough to establish educational policy as an area of class contestation and to provoke a conservative response.[14]

Weakening of an old alliance

Conditions were favourable to a right-wing counter-offensive. Labour had, by 1964, succeeded in establishing a formidable coalition of interests in support of the comprehensive school. The coalition included, of course, the working-class organisations which had traditionally supported such reform. But it also extended to sections of industry, to the educational civil service, and to the skilled and white-collar sections of the workforce whose votes were crucial to Labour's success. The ground for unity was the belief in comprehensive reform as a stimulant to economic growth, as well as a means of increasing opportunity. In the six years after 1964, one of the pillars of the alliance began to crack, while at the same time the distinct sectoral interests of some of its components became visible. As the numerous crises of the late 1960s showed, Labour's policies failed to renovate the British economy; the comprehensive school could not take its intended place as a powerful engine of economic development. At the same time, there was a growth of sectoral radicalism within education, as well as the adoption by administrators of policies such as mixed-ability teaching, markedly different from those prevalent in 1964. Thus, at the same time as one of the twin rationales of comprehensive reform was being undermined, there was a deepening of measures intended to achieve its other goal of equal opportunity. But the coalition which had initially supported change was by no means ready to support its extension in these ways: the comprehensive school seemed to be moving away from an effective workforce and a well-trained managerial and administrative cadre. These were matters of concern, not just to industry, but to many of those who had voted for Labour in 1964. Yet Labour took no political initiative that could have regained support for educational change, on a new basis. Its policies became more radical. Faced with opposition to reorganisation from Conservative LEAs it decided, for instance, to legislate to make comprehensive education universal. The problem was that this development – like the radicalism of students, teachers, etc. – was not accompanied by work to increase popular education and involvement. In fact, to a considerable extent, Labour seemed to stand back from the problems of the new comprehensives, leaving them to the experts of the sector. It is notable, for instance, that Labour in government commissioned no report on comprehensive education.

The Black Papers

The result was that opportunities were left for the right wing not just to break off the 'industrial' components of the educational alliance, but to alert middle layers of society to the dangers of further reform, and to exploit a sense of disillusionment in the working class. Such a project was initiated by the Black Papers. Polemical, often slapdash, literary essays, they ignored most issues thought central to contemporary education. They talked neither of socialisation nor of vocational training. They seemed an unlikely source for an effective critique of the dominant practices. And as a programme, they were indeed weak – it would be wrong to look to them as blueprints of an alternative model of education. As a strategy, though, for altering the balance of forces in the present, they were much stronger.

The Black Papers were less the cogent presentations of research than a series of interventions in popular debate. From this point of view, the accuracy of their research is less important than their political and ideological acuteness: their selection of targets, presentation of aims, identification of allies and choice of methods; their ability to play upon the heartstrings of those disillusioned with educational reform; and their sense of the strengths and vulnerability of their opponents. Their overall concern was with the ability of state education to produce the qualities needed by a cohesive society with an effective and cultured leadership. This meant putting an end to the influence of a particular section of state educational functionaries, by the use of methods that by-passed the normal channels of educational debate in order to appeal, through astute press campaigns, to public opinion. (To radical sectoralism they opposed conservative populism.) Their project also entailed the reinvigoration and reprogramming of the traditional defenders of educational standards and privileges; Conservatism had to be won away from the moderation of a Boyle or a Butler. Last, they required a clear and striking ideological motif that would at once inspire such a revival and show up the inadequacies of progressive ideology.

This central theme was the failure of progressive education, by which they meant the comprehensive and the Plowden primary school, to produce individuals with either an adequate basic or an advanced level of culture. The first accusation has been shown to be inaccurate, to the extent that 'basic standards', though not particularly high, have not actually declined.[15] It still, however, carries some polemical force. The second, which in many ways is more important for socialists to answer, rests on a defence of the virtues of grammar school and university, and has considerable force. Progressive education has not responded to it, stressing rather the cultivation of social qualities and the growth of the individual personality. The questions of what should be learnt, and what general cultural formation students should have, are not central to progressivism.

Whereas the Black Papers' declarations of educational objective were not at all modern, and relied heavily on the grammar school tradition, they did, in their concentration on the issue of knowledge, resound with the urgency, purpose and intellectual commitment that progressivism lacked. This central issue of their discourse was complemented by a number of subsidiary themes, all of which added to their superiority, as a combative ideology, over progressivism. Another source of potency was the sense they gave of *experience*. Whereas progressive education seemed to live in an eternal opportunistic present, taking advantage of whatever openings arose, never looking back to make critical assessments, the Black Papers claimed to bear living witness to the collapse of an experiment: the god had failed. They had lived, at first expectantly, through the moment of progressive education, and were now rejecting it from the bitter lessons of experience. Their editors were always careful to leaven the writings of timeless reactionaries with the contributions of disillusioned social democrats, such as Iris Murdoch, and Kingsley Amis, whose article, 'Why Lucky Jim Turned Right', describes the change from toleration of Labour's policies to utter hostility:

> As if moved by a fear that, despite every obstacle, a few tough customers may still emerge from the university knowing something, the Crosland illiteracy commandos get to work on the schools, chucking aside the principle of streaming which alone made the comprehensive system intelligible, and in

particular undermining the traditional sixth-form methods which saw to it that freshmen came up knowing at least the fundamentals of their subject.[16]

A verdict such as this on the inherent flaws of reform carried more weight than a backlash from the usual quarters. The Black Papers were the first balance-sheet of reform, the first testament of defection from the reforming consensus, and claimed the authenticity of the survivor's account: more did mean worse.[17]

Another asset was the ability of the Black Papers to convey a sense of crisis, a premonitary urgency, a demand for drastic remedies. In this, too, they were ahead of progressive education, which anticipated only continuing prosperity and consensus, and initially treated the Black Papers as an antediluvian freak. It was the Black Papers, and not the progressives, who highlighted problems in the schools – especially issues of discipline. Previously, as in the 'blackboard jungle' panic of the 1950s, problems of discipline had been explained as the consequence of a class-divided secondary system. It could be suggested that the comprehensive school would solve the problem. Now supporters of the Black Papers could claim that the discipline problem, like that of standards, arose from the heart of the new system. They could present their views as the result of concern for the majority of those educated. Moreover, they were able to cast their complaints in a popular form: our rights are being taken away. The concentration of reformers on influencing the state, their lack of interest in exploring the real demands and grievances of the mass of the people, meant that there was ample scope for the demagogy of the right. It was Black Paper contributors not progressives who said there was a need for a parents' movement.[18] By fostering discontent with permissive teachers, they helped to break up previous alliances.

Connectedly, they took up issues internal to educational debate – the usual province of experts – and gave them public airing in a bluff and effective way:

> the simple fact, well known to any teacher and available to all at the cost of a little reflection, that if you pack your class with thicks you will either have to ignore them and teach only the bright people or, if like most teachers you feel responsible for all

levels of pupil, you will compromise, i.e. lower your standard.[19]

However crudely expressed, such arguments, because they rested on the common sense of the age, into which progressive educational ideas had not yet percolated, had considerable effect, and met no popularly expressed critical response: mixed-ability teaching remained an esoteric and suspicious matter.

Black Papers: Right and Left compared

As strategists aiming to change the balance of forces within education, the Black Papers proved more effective than the new left. Of course, its ideas were moving with the grain; decades of routine educational conservatism eased their reception. But the new left, rather than formulating a genuinely all-round strategy, and a viewpoint from which progressive education could be judged, for long proved incapable of understanding the weakness which the Black Papers attacked, and often came out instead as progressivism's uncritical defender, leaving many important issues unanswered. It presented the Black Papers simply as the would-be restorers of privilege. The source of their appeal was not investigated. No attempt was made to present a compelling counter-definition of objectives, capable of gaining support outside educational circles. Thus, while the Black Papers were able to build themselves a base in their particular part of the educational spectrum, helping to oust a more moderate conservatism, the new left achieved no comparable success in altering the educational perspectives of the labour movement. When Callaghan accepted many of the Black Papers' criticisms, it was without significant challenge from the Labour Party. The character of the Black Papers was dynamic, shaking up and recomposing right-wing educational strategy. The response to it was less the remaking of a socialist politics of education, than of the consolidation of the left around the political perspectives of equal opportunity.[20] The practice of the new left, at the level of the school, undoubtedly went further than this; but its articulated perspectives and its strategy for winning acceptance outside the school both lagged behind. However innovatory, it had little influence, except through malevolent interpretation by the media, on popular debate about education.

William Tyndale

The clearest confrontation between new right and new left occurred at William Tyndale Junior School, Islington, in 1975.[21] The majority of teachers, including the head, championed an education that made a priority of the needs of the most disadvantaged children – rather than those from middle-class or skilled working-class homes. To do this, they reorganised the curriculum around project work and a large degree of pupil choice. They first assumed, and then demanded, the conditions of teacher autonomy that would allow this. Their reforms antagonised one teacher (a supporter of the Black Papers) who succeeded in mobilising sufficient parental opposition to the radical teachers to begin a chain of events which led to their dismissal. In fact the dismissal owed as much to the manipulations of local authority and governors as to direct parental demand. It was also assisted by an utter lack of support from the NUT. Pigs would fly, and snowballs melt in hell, declared the Chairman of the NUT's Action Committee, before the NUT offered support to the Tyndale teachers. The teachers themselves adopted weak trade-union tactics – a six-person unofficial strike – and the NUT was able to successfully stifle solidarity action with a threat of mass suspension from the union. Nevertheless, there was a specifically educational dimension to the success of the right-wing-initiated campaign, and the failure of the left (and the Tyndale teachers were hardly alone in this) to establish an effective position.

The left had a theory of learning, based on pupil motivation and self-activity. This was enough to sustain a classroom practice, but not to establish a clear set of educational objectives, defensible in terms of the advancing of working-class interests. It had the intentions of allowing 'self-realisation' and of provoking a critical attitude on the part of the students to the social demands made of them. But neither these problems, nor that of motivation, were adequately dealt with. To look for solutions only in terms of the relation between student and classroom activity opened the way to a curriculum based on the interests of the student: a method that produces, from individuals, the occasional self-realising statement, but that cannot create the entire system of sustained and various effort necessary to develop an all-round understanding of the student's society. In fact the problem of motivation has to be looked for in the relationship between the school and that section of society that is linked to it. In the 1920s, for instance, the existence of movements of working-class education, and the establishment in working-class ideology of a connection between a particular kind of knowledge and specific class interests, would have made more possible (had any radical bases then existed in the state system) the development of common educational goals among teachers, students and parents. In such a situation, motivation would have become less a matter of responding in the classroom to a pre-existing individual interest of the student, than of identifying common educational objectives, and of developing the means by which they could be attained.

The new left did not pose itself such problems. It settled for the gains available within the framework of the teacher's professional autonomy. It made little attempt to gain support for its practices even in those organisations – the NUT, the Labour Party – where some progress was possible. Nor did it carry out the systemisation of its ideas that would have been necessary to begin such an attempt. The discredited and jobless fate of the Tyndale teachers was less an evidence of their own incapacities than a warning of the dangers of a radicalism that did not step outside the classroom.

Themes of the Conservative offensive

In capturing the high ground of debate and policy, the efforts of the Black Papers were much more successful. This is not to say either that they have been largely adopted as state policy, nor that they offer an adequate outline of educational modernisation. Their very success means that the change in the direction of state policy has been interwoven over the last decade with themes largely indifferent to the relation of education to the productive process. The historic deficiencies of state policy – its toleration of a non-correspondence between education and economic need – have thus marked and impaired even the arguments of those who have helped undermine a consensus that has itself been a main agent of such asymmetry. This is true not only of the Black Papers but of the Conservative educational policy which they helped revive and redirect.

Comprehensives in question

The issue that broke the political consensus was comprehensive education. Earlier, this had seemed a matter amiably resolved. Now it became a site of permanent dispute. Circular 10/65, far from initiating a peaceful transition to universal comprehensive education, set the scene for fifteen years of conflict. Labour, in the last months of the 1964–70 government, made an unsuccessful effort to legislate for change. The next, Heath, government withdrew 10/65 and was reluctant to approve local plans for reorganisation that did not include an element of selection.[22] Throughout the fifteen years – in what was in total probably the largest 'grassroots' educational campaign of the post-war period – middle-class parents had energetically defended their grammar school. Local authorities retained selective education, in defiance of the Labour Government elected in 1974.[23] By 1976, Labour had managed to gain legal powers to enforce comprehensivisation. But the new law allowed scope for further resistance and delay. In early 1978, 70 LEAs (out of 104) still had some grammar schools. In 1979, the Conservatives repealed the law.

The strength of opposition to reorganisation was thus considerable. It involved popular resistance, ministerial and parliamentary action, and the consolidation of selective bastions: 119 direct-grant grammar schools became independent rather than be incorporated in the state sector.[24] It was noticeable that the Conservative Party was prepared to support such opposition. 'Norman St John Stevas, as the Conservatives' Shadow Education Secretary, was both promising to repeal the [1976] Act if the Conservatives won, and actively advising [LEAs] on tactics of resistance.'[25] Labour, by contrast, relied on legislation rather than mobilisation.

The intention of such activity was less to call a complete halt to comprehensive reform than to ensure that it took place in a way acceptable to Conservatives. This meant preserving some form of selection, in a variety of ways: through a strengthened private sector; through sixth-form colleges; through creating two tiers of comprehensive school, one with a sixth form, one without; through retaining a reduced number of grammar schools. In addition, the Conservatives identified particular targets they wished to knock out of the system; mixed-ability teaching and teacher-controlled exams were especially opposed. The comprehensives were also to be hedged about with measures intended to preserve inequalities between schools and to exert conformist pressure upon them.

The means to achieve this were closely worked out in opposition and, in part, implemented within eighteen months of the 1979 election. The most notorious and universally condemned measure has been the Assisted Places Scheme, which 'creams off' from twelve to fifteen thousand students a year from the state to the independent sector. A similar but less dramatic clause in the 1980 Education Act has made it the statutory duty of an LEA to pay the costs of students who live in its area but attend school in a neighbouring LEA. Thus a Conservative authority could draw students from a neighbouring comprehensive authority into its selective schools. The purpose of these measures is not simply to subsidise the private sector or allow selection to flourish. The hope is that the links established between the sectors, through which the non-selective state schools both provide preparatory education for other sectors and compete with them to attract students, will affect the character of mass education.[26]

Reaction in the curriculum

The chain of selection extends further, however, into the internal organisation of the comprehensive. Writing in opposition, both Stevas and Mark Carlisle, first Education Secretary in the 1979 Government, alleged the main problem of the comprehensive to be the proliferation of mixed-ability teaching. Carlisle wrote:

> Much of the current dissatisfaction with comprehensive schools may be traced to their internal organisation, especially mixed ability teaching. We shall therefore discourage this type of teaching and encourage schools to move towards 'setting' as the most flexible form of internal selection so as to provide adequately for the different ability groups.[27]

Stevas, more explicitly, linked a supposed decline in standards to the spread of mixed-ability teaching. He warned 'heads, governors, local authorities to be wary of allowing mixed ability teaching'. He claimed – unsurprisingly, from a viewpoint that saw differences in ability as natural and scarcely reducible – that mixed-ability teaching (MAT) was promoted 'more for ideological than for educational reasons'. On practical grounds, because MAT is 'virtually beyond most teachers' and because 'the attempt to cater for all abilities has led to an over-diversification of the curriculum', he argued that: 'Schools should have clearly defined policies for the gifted, the average and the less able . . . Separate curricula should be established for each ability group.'[28]

The second target of attack was the CSE Mode 3 examination – a type set and marked by the school, rather than by an external board. The effect of Mode 3 has been to broaden the range of subjects, to relate classroom work more closely to students' interests, to allow mixed-ability work in the fourth and fifth years of the school, and to open up at least the possibility of courses that develop a critical attitude to the object of study. For Stevas, Mode 3 led away from education in basic skills towards an unacceptable diversification of the curriculum. It also 'raised doubts in some people's minds' – he later referred to parents and employers – 'about the whole value of CSE'.[29]

The targets and intentions of attack were very much those identified by contributors to the Black Papers. The specific measures taken by the Thatcher Government, however, were less radical than those proposed in opposition. In April 1979, for instance, Carlisle could endorse Black Paper demands to 'set up national standards in reading, writing and arithmetic. These standards would be set up by the APU and monitored by a bank of tests at set ages.'[30] In government, no such step was taken. To standardise the curriculum in this way, to reduce it largely to activities that can be measured by a bank of tests, and to end local autonomy, would challenge beliefs and practices that are deeply rooted in the education system. Since the Conservative Government did not want a confrontation with almost the entire apparatus of state education, it refrained from devising any bill to establish 'national standards'. Thus, although the targets identified by the Black Papers remained still in Conservative sights, the methods of attack used were substantially different. There was little direct intervention in the school curriculum. Discussion documents were issued on a 'Framework for the Curriculum', and the setting up of a unified system of examination at 16+ was postponed and heavily modified.

Parents as a market force

Otherwise, the line of attack was indirect. Here, too, it drew from the Black Papers' strategic armoury. A contributor to Black Paper 1977 wrote:

> A nation-wide Parent Teacher Association, to which both parents and teachers who are concerned about the debasement of education can appeal for help and protection against victimisation is possibly what is most urgently needed today . . . The parent movement is the significant force that is emerging to shake the foundations of the bureaucratic educational pyramid at its broad base.[31]

It was to parental choice that the Thatcher Government turned as a conservatising influence. Carlisle promised to introduce legislation:

> embodying our Parents' Charter. This will place a clear obligation . . . local authorities to take account of parents' wishes when allocating children to schools, and will require all schools to publish prospectuses giving details of their examinations and other results.[32]

'Parents' Charter' was rather a demagogic expression. The populist perspectives of 'building a movement against the debasement of education' were not fulfilled by Carlisle's Education Act. Nevertheless, parental choice is a significant weapon. By forcing schools, in a context of falling rolls and possible closure, to compete for favour before a parental audience schooled in the virtues of basic education and higher standards, Carlisle did more than impose a set of legislative changes. He cleared the ground for a steady conservatising pressure to be exerted on comprehensive schools, discouraging them from untoward experiment. Such pressure is all the more difficult to resist since it is not based on any parental involvement in the discussion of educational aims. It is the influence of the market, of the aggregation of individual consumer demand, and not the pressure of an organised parental movement in possible but unwanted dialogue with teachers, that is intended to keep the school in line.

School, work and unemployment: Conservative policy

Whatever the success of such an approach in reinforcing pressure on the schools, it does not address itself to the relationship between education and the economy. In opposition, the Conservatives, like the Black Papers, were most animated by the threat of egalitarianism. The lengthy campaigns against comprehensive education and the careful preparation of the 1980 Act were not matched by a similarly detailed concern for the issues highlighted by the OECD report and the (Labour) Green Paper.

Developments since 1979 have forced a redirection of concern, without changing the basic emphases of Conservative policy. In office, the Conservatives, like Labour before them, were forced to attend to the accumulated weakness of English education in the area of the training of a workforce. Crowther had recommended, twenty years previously – and in the spirit of the 1918 Education Act – that full-time education to 16, and part-time education to 18, should be provided for all. As in 1918, this was not a suggestion that was implemented; there were no moves to establish an integrated system of education and training.[33] Instead, there remained throughout the 1960s and 1970s a chaos of disparate courses and qualifications. At the same time, on-the-job industrial training – provided by the firm, not the state – declined sharply. In 1968 there were over 300,000 young workers involved in such training – a number that by 1981 had fallen below 90,000.[34] Meanwhile, school sixth forms, under the stimulus of university expansion, grew considerably. The decline in industrial training was a result partly of recession and de-industrialisation, and partly of a change in the character of work – a change that led the government 'Think Tank' to argue in 1980 that 'the concept of skill and in particular apprenticeship has more to do with trade-union restrictive practices than with the needs of modern industry'.[35] Superimposed on these developments was the vast growth in youth unemployment, to the extent that, without government intervention in the form of 'training' schemes, over 50 per cent of 16- and 17-year-olds would be jobless.[36]

Thus the growing concern over the lack of a 'technical' orientation in English education became increasingly intertwined with problems of mass youth unemployment and 'deskilling' changes in the nature of work. The combination gave rise to educational initiatives which have oscillated between proclamation of the need for a general restructuring of education so as to produce new skills, and a practical settling for a more limited kind of pre-vocational training, which emphasises adjustment to economic restructuring and states more firmly the need for schools – and other institutions – to create in students a more appropriate attitude to work and/or unemployment. Such an outlook is detectable not only in post-Great Debate policy, but in aspects of Crowther and Newsom. The difference is one of degree: the educational system is now being substantially remodelled to meet the needs that earlier reports discussed, but were able to do little about.

Conservative education policy in government adapted itself to these requirements, while preserving the 'defence of excellence' which it championed in opposition. Keith Joseph, as Secretary of State, made clear his intention to maintain traditional – that is, academic and selective – sixth forms in most places where they were threatened by tertiary reorganisation. Likewise, there was little encouragement for suggestions that the 'A' Level system should be modified. On the other hand, the Conservative Government adjusted rapidly to the problems of youth unemployment. The DES introduced a 17 + 'pre-vocational certificate' to keep some of the unemployed at school. Others will be enrolled in the Manpower Services Commission youth-training schemes. Observers commented that the reform of courses which is under way did not seem to be motivated by consideration of the need for high levels of skill: unemployment, de-industrialisation and de-skilling do not require advanced forms of training.[37]

Thus, although originating from the kind of awareness promoted by the OECD report, Conservative policy came little closer to evolving the kind of systematic industrial training recommended by the OECD. To do so would have run counter to the priorities of government economic policy, which did not involve widespread programmes of industrial regeneration.

Equality and efficiency?

The Labour Party, on the other hand, argued for economic expansion, and wanted education to have a major role in industrial recovery. In keeping with its traditional coupling of equality with efficiency, it asserted that the goals of reform and those of economic survival are compatible. 'We must ensure', said Neil Kinnock, that education 'gains the importance of economic, industrial and energy policy. That is an elementary necessity if we are to make our society more harmonious, more articulate, more reasoning, more tolerant, more democratic. That is a fundamental priority if we are to survive economically.'[38] The Labour Party's 1982 discussion document on 16–19 education thus extended the principle of equal opportunity into a relatively new area, pointing out that 'by far the highest proportion of young people who continue in full or part-time education after the age of 16 are still from middle-class backgrounds'.[39] To change the situation, Labour pledged to reorganise 16–19 education on a comprehensive basis, with a statutory right of access. These proposed reforms, if implemented, would represent progress, and should be supported. I would argue, though, that they avoid questions arising from Labour's past record, from the nature of the present economic restructuring, and from the nature of the present systems of post-16 training.

From Callaghan's 1976 speech onwards, the achievements of his government were to give comfort to the educational reactionaries whom Callaghan was echoing, and to license developments pointing towards an education system firmly linked to conceptions of national need acceptable to industry and the IMF. Circulars from the DES, under Labour, laid down quite openly the ideological requirements that industry made of schools. Chief Education Officers, for instance, received in 1978 a document 'setting out the part that schools can play in the government's industrial strategy'. This included 'preparing pupils more effectively while at school for the transition to adult and working life, in particular by equipping them with a basic understanding of the functioning of the economy and of activities, especially manufacturing, which create the nation's wealth'.[40] It was Labour, too, that from 1974 developed the Manpower Services Commission (MSC), a body that has played a major part in the restructuring of

educational spending and planning. In 1982 it spent £1,000 million
a year, and had a staff of 22,000. The courses it has planned, under
Conservative and Labour governments, have been models of
palliative and low-skill training, with almost no general educational
content.

The Labour Party's document certainly differs from the policy
of Callaghan's government in its rediscovery of a reforming zeal.
Yet it leaves several questions unanswered. It makes no assessment
of Labour's record. Nor does it consider how, once the legitimacy
of industrial demand is unequivocally admitted, it is possible to
resist pressures for types of education that prioritise the school's
adjustment to the technical and ideological needs of a productive
system in considerable crisis. Labour may well claim that its
establishment of a universal and statutory system is greatly superior
to Youth Opportunities Programme schemes reliant upon the
goodwill of the employer, but its educational objectives do not
seem to be greatly different from those of the MSC. It has not
begun to develop socialist responses to the awkward questions
provoked by crisis: What is the function of mass post-16 education
at a time of mass youth unemployment? How will Labour
counteract the demands of the job market for a relatively low-
skilled workforce, schooled in the virtues of adaptability?

The questions are not at all academic. Initiatives intended to
realise equal opportunity have a way of being pulled out of shape
by the steady imperatives of the economic system. Such influences,
upon pre-vocational education, will be all the heavier. And if
Labour commits itself to an extension of post-16 education which
turns out not to differ significantly in its relation to the labour
market from earlier efforts, then it will see reproduced on a larger
scale the popular dissatisfaction that characterised the later years of
comprehensive reform.

With Labour in power?

I would argue, then, that the development of a *popular* programme
of reform is dependent upon Labour being willing to tackle
questions of the purpose and content of education, from a
perspective that challenges the industrially related priorities that
now influence the planning of structure and curriculum. This also

implies, of course, a policy towards the ownership and control of capital radically different from that of previous Labour governments.

Without the ability to mobilise support, it is likely not just that Labour's programme of 16–19 reform will be limited, but also that the attacks on privilege to which it is now committed will meet obstacles of a possibly insurmountable kind. If, for instance, a Labour government attempts a policy that effectively closes down the public schools, it will face determined resistance. The public schools will respond with a campaign that questions the international legality of their abolition, in breach of the UN Charter of Human Rights. It would not be surprising if they gained the approval of the courts for such an argument. They will also be able to rely, as in the past, on the obstructiveness of a civil service, a large part of which was itself privately educated. All this, of course, will be accompanied by a militant ideological defence of individual freedom, not without public resonance. To be able to proceed towards their abolition, Labour will have to be able to arouse deep popular opposition to the public schools. This depends, in turn, on Labour's ability to win assent to a new definition of educational objectives, based at the very least on support for comprehensive and progressive gains. Labour's present educational politics are in no state to allow the easy realisation of such an achievement, and no important body of the labour and trade-union movement is capable of devising alternatives.

Trade-union weakness

This was shown by the response of the labour movement and of the educational left to the 'Great Debate'. The TUC favoured its new stresses; there was some preliminary welcome for the 'spirit of enquiry' that progressive educational change had fostered – but the central point was unmistakable: 'At the same time, the nation must not fail to harness the intellect, the skill and experience and the imagination of all our workers in improving economic performance.'[41] Two years later, Len Murray confirmed this approach: 'We will be looking for practical measures from this [Conservative] government to encourage new methods and forms of teaching about industrial society.'[42] The NUT, more defensively, argued that schooling's closer relationship to manpower needs:

> could lead both to unprecedented interference in the work of schools, and to a very narrow view of the purpose and content of education. We believe that the nation's economic and social interests are best served when education develops the talents and abilities of the people to the fullest and widest extent.[43]

These are no more than the platitudes of the 1960s. The NUT pledged its loyalties, albeit a little uncritically, to the world of work, while being unable to describe convincingly the steps that education should take towards it. It thus lay stranded, neither critic nor vehicle of the proposed changes.

Its claim of an area of activity – the curriculum – as the legitimate realm of teacher autonomy was likewise disabling. While for the DES the issue of curriculum control was linked to and prepared by a debate on educational goals and methods, the NUT too frequently addressed the problem in terms of the single issue of control, attempting to extract it from the complex of issues in which it was embedded. The desire to increase teachers' professional influence led the NUT to centre its comments on the need for the union to have 'formal association with . . . the official planning activities of the DES'.[44] The corollary of this plea was, of course, a professional jealousy of any outside interference – industrial, parental, trade-union – in the teachers' work.

When educational objectives were discussed, it was only in terms of the behavioural attainments of individual students. 'Mature, responsible, literate and numerate young people'; 'mature, thinking, young, adults'; 'the development of a person's self-awareness'; 'The obligation to provide the school-leaver with life skills . . . and to look at the personal development of the individual' – all these nebulous phrases are taken from the NUT's contribution to the 'Great Debate'.[45]

The Left: missing the point

Those academics and writers associated with educational reform were similarly unable to deal with the 'school–work' connection.

Like the NUT, their response has settled on legitimate but secondary issues: the demonstration that standards have not fallen; refutation of standardised testing; objection to central control of the curriculum. All these are points worth making; none was central. The basic line of state policy-making ran from the OECD report, through the two House of Commons committees on DES policy-making and the achievements of the school-leaver, to the 'Great Debate' and Green Paper and the circulars of curricular guidance sent out by the DES. By contrast, in the work of the major defenders of reform – Brian Simon's numerous articles, Nigel Wright's *Progress in Education*, Dennis Lawton's *The Politics of the School Curriculum*[46] – no such considerations centrally appear. To have responded critically to the theme of school and work would have required a quite fundamental explanation and rejection of the effects of the division of labour upon the work of the school. As we have seen, such qualities were not available in progressive or labour traditions.

Nor, though, were they evident in the activity of avowed militant socialists. A typical response was ignorance: at the time of the OECD report, trade-union tactics were the main debate on the organised left. The first response of *Rank and File Teacher* to the 'Great Debate' was to dismiss it as a 'smokescreen for the cuts'.[47] Later, there was some discussion of its connection with the 'needs of industry' but not of the crisis afflicting traditional strategies and ideologies of reform. Elsewhere – in *Socialist Teacher* and *Radical Education* for instance – there was more awareness of what was at stake. The basic disabling assumptions of progressive and professional attitudes were sketched and criticised. Even so, their response did not develop much beyond the point of defence of those aspects of progressive education most under attack, and limited initiatives on curricular issues: anti-racism, anti-sexism, international struggles. Though such developments were radical and welcome, they could not in themselves constitute a complete break from the progressive framework – they remained a form of sectoral educational militancy. Nor could they provide an alternative presentation of the relation between education and production to that embodied in state policy. Rather than attempting to work out a socialist approach to the problem, the tendency was to write off the whole issue as a product of reaction. Such discussion as there was on these topics occurred in the last years of Callaghan's government. Since 1979 there has been a stress on basic defensive struggles against cuts in educational provision and a disheartening neglect of the broader issues.

These various responses are sufficient to allow us to speak without exaggeration of a crisis in educational policy, which extends from the traditional reforming strategy through to the far left in the trade unions. It is thus a rather bleak prospect that stretches in front of the educational left. To answer the most pressing questions requires considerable advance upon past practice. This is the case not only for those who have been in the mainstream of the reforming tradition, but also those who have kept something of a critical distance from it. It is their practice that is reviewed in the following chapter.

5

Socialist alternatives

In attempting to develop an alternative to the main strategies of reform, the left – that is to say, those socialists who stand even partly outside a tradition of state-orientated reform – does not completely lack precedent. There have been numerous encounters between such socialists and the main aspects of the reforming tradition: progressive education, equal opportunity, teacher professionalism. The patterns of strength and weakness revealed in these encounters are fairly regular. It is worth examining them so as to learn from the re-posing of old questions, and to recognise weaknesses that have typified the left's response to them.

In this history, since 1918, there have been two periods of independent activity and one, largely, of silence. Between 1918 and 1935 there were sustained efforts, led by the Communist Party and influenced by workers' education movements, to develop a revolutionary socialist critique of state education and of its reformers. From the mid-1930s to, roughly, 1968, socialists were submerged in the fight for equal opportunity, aspiring to be the best fighters for reform. Since 1968 there has been a re-emergence of explicitly socialist attitudes, centred upon militant trade unionism and on a curricular radicalism which tends to identify, once again, state education as a hostile system that requires transformation, rather than as a benign force whose chief need is expansion.

The Teachers' Labour League

Since the early years of the Labour Party there had been attempts to 'win teachers for Labour'. Such attempts were directed to winning teachers to *voting* for Labour, rather than to developing a socialist presence within the school system. It was not until after the First World War that the project of developing the teacher constituency was combined with an active, sectoral politics of education. The main organisation responsible for the combined political effort was the Teachers' Labour League (TLL). The TLL's fifteen-year existence was marked by abrupt shifts in its nature and objectives. It arose at the end of the war from the electoral growth of Labour, from a renewed economic militancy, and from the debate on party affiliation that divided the NUT in 1919. Initially, it sought only to 'lead teachers to Labour by the quietest methods'.[1] Its sponsors, who included Russell, Wells and Tawney, were drawn from the respectable Labour intelligentsia. However, the TLL was affected by the ideas of currents outside the Labour Party – such as the Plebs League – which challenged assumptions that the path of progress lay in a largely quantitative growth of education. It was this critique of state education that its activists, who soon included members of the then unproscribed Communist Party, took up. By 1926, when it produced its first regular publication, *Educational Worker*, its politics were aligned with the left of the labour movement, and were strongly influenced by the Communist Party. It affiliated to the Educational Workers' International (EWI), a body informally linked to the Communist Third International. Its orientation was now markedly non-electoral; it was more concerned with organising a socialist tendency in the teaching unions and with popularising a critique of state education.

A distance developed between the League and its official backers. While Tawney, for instance, sat on advisory committees of the Board of Education, other TLL members, delegates to an EWI conference in Vienna, were trailed by the Special Branch.[2] The tensions between such different orientations produced a split. In 1927 the TLL's leading public figures – MPs, members of the Labour ACE and the NUT Executive – walked out of its Annual General Meeting. The League was swiftly expelled from the Labour Party and an alternative official body, the National Association of

Labour Teachers (NALT), was set up. This was not the end of the TLL, but was, nevertheless, an eventually crucial setback.

The TLL was one of the first active socialist organisations of state employees in Britain. As such its experience is of continuing interest. It represented an attempt to give local relevance to the educational gains of the Russian Revolution. It attempted, in the process, a critique of progressive education. It tried to relate the critiques of the 'independent working-class education' movement to the state sector, and in doing so developed an alternative 'line' to that of the Labour Party's educational policy-makers. In all these incomplete and often rudimentary efforts it offers us, even now, a model at least of the *areas* of activity that a socialist educational tendency should address.

USSR: the polytechnic school

In its most productive phase, the League's greatest strength was its international affiliation. The EWI was no international assembly of grouplets, but a body that included major teaching unions in France, Germany and the USSR. Although some of the most sophisticated theoretical work was German,[3] the overwhelming concern of the EWI was in popularising the educational practice of the Soviet Union. Soviet education was, at least during the early 1920s, a vast, if impoverished field of experimentation, whose achievements and perspectives provided a basis for criticisms of the aims, method and content of Western education. In a number of ways it had broken decisively from Western conceptions of mass education. Most important, it had been set the objective of developing a high level of general culture, sufficient to allow, among other things, the informed participation of the population in the affairs of state. The student was not to be the recipient of a merely technical education; as Lunacharsky, first People's Commissar for Education, didactically put it:

The finest conquest of Communism will be a renaissance of art and of the sciences – this is the most sublime objective of human evolution. Marx told us that the only goal worthy of humanity is the greatest possible enlargement of all human faculties.[4]

Such a statement could have been dismissed as an official humanist gloss on a system that in practice denied such values, had it not been for the attempts made to embody its ambitions, if in less glamorous form, in the curriculum of Soviet schools. The aim was to provide:

> general preparation and general study of the work necessary for each adolescent, independent of the profession or trade that he will choose in the future. As the greatest common divisor, this sum will appear in all of the professions, in all of the skilled work, thus representing the minimum of knowledge necessary before beginning to learn a profession or trade.[5]

What this entailed in practice is shown by an educational programme generally adopted in 1923, and intended for 14-year-old students:

a.   *Nature and Man*

1.   Sufficient physics and chemistry to understand:
A.   The lives of men and animals
B.   The application of these sciences in industry (construction of machines and motors, electricity, etc.)
2.   Minerals, mines, combustibles. Russian mineral regions and coalfields . . .

b.   *Work*

1.   The extraction of minerals and combustibles.
2.   Chemical and mechanical industry. Hand work, manufacturing, factory industry. Organisation of work in a small shop, in a factory and in a manufacturing plant. The development of different branches of industry in Russia and in other countries . . .
3.   Technology of agricultural production.
4.   Anthropological geography . . .
5.   Man as a worker. The organisation of his work . . .

c.   *Society*

The workers and the capitalists. Wage labour and capital. Private property and labour. The situation of the working class. The union of aristocrats and capitalists . . . Trade unions. Political parties. Capitalism in Russia. Survivals of Feudalism. Monarchy.[6]

Despite the propagandist tone of some of this course (understandable in the context of the early Soviet State), and despite its gaps in the aesthetic areas specified by Lunacharsky, it still represents an effort to deliver a general knowledge of society. It is arguable that, of the three general headings, 'nature and man', 'labour' and 'society', the latter two are still not subjects of inquiry at any comparable stage of English education.

Discipline and teaching methods were also related to overall education aims:

> The difference which exists between the objects that we propose for the school and those that the bourgeois state proposes, exercise a decisive influence on the form and the object of student autonomy . . . In our schools, self-government is not a means of governing the students more readily, neither is it a practical method for studying the workings of the constitution. It is a means by which the pupils may learn to live and to work intelligently.[7]

The students were expected to organise 'economic, recreational and artistic work' as well as 'surveillance' of teachers' work, collective discipline, and day-to-day tasks of minor administration. The duty of the teacher was to consist in 'actively contributing to student autonomy'. Educational methods were based on group investigation of 'complexes of inquiry' rather than on whole-class teaching or individual project work. The intention was not merely to set up a vocational system of education, or a system of handicraft, but to study, through practical participation, a whole system of production, and to examine its forms of political control. This was described as 'polytechnic education'. As defined by Nadezhda Krupskaya, one of its main theorists, it:

> had the aim of studying modern technology in general, its main achievements and its foundations, the inter-relationships between the various branches of production and development tendencies of modern technology. It aims to show where this

development is leading us . . . The worker is not just somebody who carries out orders here. Today he carries out orders, tomorrow he can be an inventor, and the day after tomorrow an important organiser in a factory.[8]

Children, then, should learn by taking part in work and social life. As one summary puts it:

Teachers were encouraged to take the problems of the children, of local production and of daily life as their starting point, and to examine them in the light of various disciplines simultaneously. Instead of learning geography or history children were, for instance, to study the village they lived in by taking part in work, talking to farmers and workers and the like.[9]

This experience, which combined new approaches to curriculum, pedagogy, discipline and to the relationship between school and work, was not, it is true, ever developed in the context of a society with a highly developed division of labour. It was applied in largely rural areas, or in relation to workshops, where investigation of methods of production and of social relations was easier. Nor did it deal with problems of higher-level education. Nevertheless, it offered a basis from which to criticise not only the dominant forms of state education in the West, but also the progressive alternatives to them. As we shall see, however, in England the opportunity was less than half-grasped.

Britain: knowledge is power

A more immediate and powerful influence upon the TLL was provided by the movements of 'independent working-class education'. The strongest of these was the Plebs League which was quite firmly based in the most militant sections of the working class: miners, railway workers, dockers, engineers. We have already seen that the content of its classes attracted the attention of government Intelligence. But it would be wrong to see the Plebs League, or the National Council of Labour Colleges, as purely educational organisations. They were, rather, offshoots of the militant socialism that developed, on either side of the First World

War, outside the bounds of Labour politics. In contrast to later forms of trade-union education, the Plebs League was not especially concerned with providing training in the skills of negotiation and administration. Education was, rather, a weapon of central importance in the class struggle: 'Knowledge is Power'. The Plebs and its counterparts aimed to create an informed, working-class minority, capable of interpreting history, politics and economics from a class-conscious viewpoint. It was hostile to the efforts of organisations like the Workers' Educational Association to educate and civilise the working class through making more widely available the benefits of the dominant culture. In all this, it was not an accidental by-product of the crisis of the 1920s, but an influential current, the culmination of efforts by socialist militants to educate not just individuals, eccentric by virtue of their self-education, but a layer of the working class, equipping it with knowledge useful in the struggle for political power.[10] This current did not make a priority of intervening in state education. It fell to the Teachers' Labour League to direct some of the energies set in motion by the Plebs League into criticising the state school, and to utilise its implacably class-conscious insights in developing an alternative to Labour's educational programme.

Teachers

The TLL operated, briefly, in a context in which teachers were receptive to radicalism and to the aims of Soviet education. English teachers in the early 1920s were in political and organisational turmoil. The largest union, the NUT, had been shaken by local strikes over pay, by an intense debate on affiliation to the Labour Party, in which proposals to affiliate were lost only by a two-to-one margin, and by sexual divisions arising from the equal-pay issue. This latter dispute led to the consciously feminist secession of the National Union of Women Teachers (NUWT) from the NUT and the setting up of a new, consciously male union, the National Association of Schoolmasters (NAS).[11] Strikes, and the Labour Party agitation, called into question the union's traditional renunciation of trade-union methods and of open politics. At the same time, there was a strong element of moral protest against the education system's contribution to war, and a realisation that the old education could not continue. Political and progressive-educational influences were strong, also, in the NUWT, which was much bolder than the NUT in relating to issues like that of suffrage, and to near-pacifist anti-war campaigning.[12] The early 1920s were also the highpoint of the influence of progressive education in its most radical phase. Critiques of the barbarity of state education were at their sharpest; progressive experiments mushroomed both outside the state sector and within it.[13]

Radicalism was thus present (in different forms) to some extent among teachers' organisations, in debate about the school régime, and in the working-class movement. State reform, on the other hand, seemed paralysed: despite frequent calls for a renewal of state education, so as to counter the influence of the independent working-class movement, the 'Fisher Act' of 1918 had been left largely unimplemented, and such progress as existed was molecular. For a few years at the beginning of the 1920s it seemed possible that a unified and powerful socialist movement could establish a real hegemony among the working class. What part did the TLL have in developing the potential of such a movement?

TLL agitation

It was at its strongest in criticising, in words and action, the policy of the Labour Party. The first issue of *Educational Worker* carried a critical review of the latest Labour policy document: it was 'a series of excellent suggestions for [education's] improvement and extension . . . but surely not a policy and still less a Labour policy! Not a word about the aims of education; not a word about the control of educational policy.'[14] As good as its word, the League took up the issue of control, involving parents and school students in protest against Empire Day.[15] It helped set up 'Workers' Councils on Education' – whose national president was the miners' leader A. J. Cook – to investigate class bias in the schools and to campaign against caning, scouting (seen as a vehicle for imperialist propaganda), and biased textbooks.[16]

It thus campaigned not simply for the expansion of state education but against its most obnoxious features. It combined this not with uncritical identification with progressive education, but with an attempt to debate with progressives their assumptions of the school's role. The major way in which it tried to counterpose socialist to progressive education was through debating the issue 'neutral versus class-conscious education'. The debate originated in international differences within the EWI.[17] 'L'école n'est pas au service d'une classe, elle est au service de l'enfant', declared the French delegation to the first conference of the EWI. The writer Romain Rolland argued in the EWI's first bulletin, 'The sacred mission of the school is to form strong personalities and free intelligences . . . All clericalism – bourgeois or proletarian – is the enemy.'[18] The situating of education's psychological objectives outside of discussion of its social goals was a characteristic of progressivism. The TLL faced a similar tendency in England. A. S. Neill's views on the 'spiritual' nature of the East End problem, aired in this debate, have already been quoted. The League, by referring to the Russian example, aimed to show that educational goals could only be defined and defended in the context of a clear social commitment.

Perhaps most important, the League aimed to make such ideas – among others – the basis of a grouping of socialist activists in the NUT and NUWT. It thus had to accompany its propaganda and critiques with a specific programme of agitation that addressed the major questions facing teachers: pay, education cuts, the employers' repression, democratic reform. On all of these issues it emphasised that without an alliance with the working class the teachers' cause was doomed. The cornerstone of a socialist strategy among teachers had to include, at its centre, the question of such an alliance.

In this area the League enjoyed a virtual monopoly: the NALT was uninterested in agitation, preferring to develop the outlines of a future government policy. The TLL, therefore, could occasionally attract large audiences. Seven hundred attended its meeting at the 1928 NUT Conference[19] where Cook, a leading figure on the left, spoke. The League was thus able to gain some support in its fight for limited, democratic reforms. Here, though, it found its way blocked by the Labour Party teachers. At the 1929 NUT Conference, a leading NALT member, Leah Manning, attacked the TLL's proposal for the secularisation of the school, pleading the 'valued opportunities to teach religion pure and undefiled to the little children'.[20]

Failure and decline

It is clear, then, that the TLL was rather more than a tendency which occupied itself with routine trade-union agitation, or with a concentration on refining policies that would be implemented at some future date by a sympathetic government. It instead aimed to win teachers to an alliance with the working-class movement that extended beyond the electoral field. The alliance involved, certainly, joint action on economic questions, but had also an important educational dimension: it was necessary to win teachers not simply to support various criticisms of the present system, but also to endorse a socialist analysis of the system's *raison d'être*, and of alternatives to it. Such an objective was in several ways a novel one: in its attempts to influence an important group of state employees; in its combining of economic and ideological agitation; in its international scope; and in its efforts to engage with the most advanced systems of non-socialist educational thought. Its work should remind us that a politics of education is a politics in the widest sense, addressing questions of state policy, posing strategic alliances, alert to political developments outside the sector and criticising particular ideological currents within it. The League's efforts remain salutary. The paths that, because of its connections with the international communist movement and with a socialist tendency in the British working class, it was able to suggest are ones that the left in contemporary education needs to develop.

Yet it failed. Through a combination of hostile circumstances and its own deficiences, it established neither an immediate strength nor a lasting influence. Its own weaknesses are matters for later discussion; the context of its failure needs to be outlined here, since with it were installed conditions that inhibited socialist advance for the next four decades.

The post-1918 growth of the Labour Party, as well as being an important advance, also set in motion a gradual assimilation of areas that had once been the ground of independent working-class activity into a politics that was firmly directed towards administering the existing state. The great rise in the Labour vote, and the party's increased access to local and national administration, meant that a layer of the party became both educated in running the system, and influenced by its existing procedures. This layer, transmitting its ideas and exercising its power throughout the labour movement, formed a powerful opposition to ideas that had previously run tolerantly parallel with those of equal opportunity, but were now seen as incompatible.

Likewise, the calming of the post-war turbulence among teachers increased their distance from the working class. The setting up of a national committee (Burnham) to negotiate salaries ended local pay disputes, the main focuses of militancy. Sexual divisions in teaching were sharpened by the equal-pay issue. The NUT, while supporting the idea in principle, did nothing to fight for it in practice. It also accepted that, upon marriage, a woman teacher should lose her job. These policies ensured the existence of an underclass of women teachers, paid at three-quarters the rate of men and holding what was in effect only temporary status. The formation of the NAS made matters worse. It was opposed on principle to equal pay and tried to raise salaries by cutting teacher supply, through the expulsion of women from the workforce. Its objects were plain: 'to safeguard and promote the interests of men teachers'.[21]

In these circumstances the brief post-war gains in consciousness were rolled back. 'It would be futile to deny', wrote the TLL in 1927, 'the hostility that many teachers feel towards working class struggles.'[22] The NUT's newspaper welcomed the end of the General Strike ('the great ordeal') and printed a message to teachers from the President of the Board, congratulating them on 'their devoted and successful attempts to carry on their duties . . . contributing to stability and orderliness'.[23] Its next issue reported that in the East End only twenty out of 1,200 teachers had failed to report for work during the strike, though some had been turned out of their cars by 'irresponsible gangs of people who had chosen this method of protest against all traffic'.[24] The political attitudes implied in such articles were taken into the classroom. Even in a strongly socialist area such as the Rhondda, children who wore communist badges, or refused to stand for the (English) national anthem, could expect to be beaten.[25] Although during the 1920s NUT opinion came to disapprove of the extremes of nationalist ritual, it did not regard the celebration of Empire Day as anything but proper. Such conservatism was sustained by some deliberately granted improvements in teachers' material position: a national minimum wage, a pension structure, greater freedom from supervision by inspectors and governors. Teachers' enhanced status and security is measured by the NUT's historian in the increasing numbers of magistrates, councillors and MPs produced from their ranks.[26] It can also be demonstrated by the statistics of union membership. While the size of the Miners' Federation fell by half, to 500,000, between 1920 and 1930, the NUT's numbers rose from 115,000 to 144,000.[27] This recruitment was based less on militancy than on the union's success in obtaining limited professional gains from a state anxious to prevent teacher radicalism.[28] Professional improvement and working-class advance did not seem necessarily related.

The defeat of the General Strike widened such divisions. After 1926, to hope for gains to be made through direct action in contestation with the state seemed utopian. The Plebs tradition went into decline; the restructuring of state education which began with the Hadow Report seemed to offer a more realistic perspective of change. The aggressive measures taken by Baldwin's Government after 1926 were matched by those of the labour bureaucracies. The expulsion of the TLL from the Labour Party was one of many defeats which confirmed the isolation of the most militant sections of the working class.

International problems . . .

At the same time, changes in Soviet education and international communist politics weakened the League. In an isolated and impoverished workers' state, it was always likely that the difficult aim of educating a citizenry capable of democratic involvement in national politics and economic planning would be challenged by a perspective that sought the quickest route to industrialisation: a skilled but narrowly educated workforce, coercively led by a ruling group whose decisions were not open to political challenge. These tensions were present even in the early days of polytechnic education, and a growing vocationalism had altered the initial emphasis on a broad formative education. By the late 1920s – the beginning of Stalin's dominance – the vocational tendencies had been strengthened. Forced collectivisation in the countryside, a hectic programme of industrialisation, and the growing use of political terror against political opponents discouraged education's enquiry into the mechanisms of social life. The repression of dissent dictated a régime of conformity in the school; the partial self-government practised in the early 1920s came to an end. The need to develop specialist 'cadres' to implement an industrialisation carried through without regard for political opposition led not only to an increasing stress on the purely technical aspects of education, but to an eradication of the earlier contents and methods of Soviet education.

Such developments, with their stress on conformity, obedience, technical skill above general culture, and mass literacy, were in line with many aspects of Western education. The new emphasis on these qualities robbed communists of a body of experiment and achievement that had previously given them a means of critically judging the capitalist school. At the same time it strengthened the pressure upon communists to make some accommodation with what was now, after all, a not-so-dissimilar system.

These were some of the long-term effects of Soviet development. But in the short term, their influence was obscured by the consequences of the sharp political turn made by the Communist International. In 1928, Stalin announced a new perspective: post-war capitalism had allegedly entered a 'Third Period' of catastrophic collapse which would, it was argued, lead to mass political radicalisation. In its death throes, capitalism was transforming the political system in an effort to find a last desperate means of defence. One such means was Fascism. Another was said to be the transformation of Social Democratic parties into organisations that devoted themselves to the last-ditch defence of the capitalist order: 'Social Democracy' wrote Stalin, 'is the moderate wing of Fascism . . . These organisations do not negate but complement each other.'[29]

. . . and local consequences

In Britain, the practical consequence of such a line was to deepen the split between Communists and the rest of the labour movement. The TLL wrote, in October 1929, that the Labour Party was not a working-class party and that the NUT had now become 'part and parcel of the capitalist state machine'.[30] By June 1930 it had decided that 'the TLL is destined to become the Educational Workers Trade Union'.[31] Such sectarianism, and such a bad misreading of the political situation, threw the TLL into crisis. It declined into becoming the 'teachers' section' of the Communist Party, which itself was losing members fast. There was, at the end of 1930, an attempt to reorientate the League's politics on a more realistic course, but the redrafting of its aims which then took place was, if anything, even more revealing of the organisation's decline. A 'united front' approach to militants in the Labour Party was ruled out, and the educational dimension of policy was seen largely as an irrelevancy. The intention now was to centre activity on 'real and practical demands'[32] which showed up the 'betrayal by the Labour Party of the interests of the working class'. Whatever ability Labour might once have had to deliver reforms was by now exhausted. In education this meant that Labour could no longer pursue even the moderate demands that were historically its own. One of the best ways, therefore, of 'exposing' social democracy was to take over its demands and show that it would not fight for them. The radicalising masses would then recognise the Communist Party as the real fighters.

In this way a theory asserting the automatic connection between economic crisis and political militancy allowed the fight for reforms to be presented as a programme for socialism, 'topped off' by the assertion that only a workers' government would carry them out. The educational component of the TLL's work dwindled away. In future the Labour Party's educational programme, which had neither collapsed, nor was exposed, enjoyed unchallenged dominance.

The Left and reform (1933–68)

The 'Third Period's' heyday did not last beyond 1933, when the debacle of the German Communist Party before Hitler forced the adoption of a new strategy. Increasingly, and especially after 1935, communist parties adopted the policies of the Popular Front, of the unity of all democratic forces, socialist, communist or bourgeois, against the threat of Fascism. The sectarianism of the previous years was thus mostly abandoned. The new line established a pattern of strategy that was to endure for more than thirty years. Its essential problem was the subordination of specifically socialist policies to the needs of a broad democratic alliance. As one critic put it, 'The Communists, in order to give their desired allies of the "democratic bougeoisie" nothing to fear from a joint fight against fascism, systematically opposed the formulation of objectives of a socialist type.'[33] This general approach had consequences for the education policy of the English Communists. The 1930s saw the construction of an alliance, which included forces well to the right of the labour movement, that pressed for the expansion of education. Increasingly, government-commissioned reports, like that of Spens, began to consider ending some of the more blatant inequalities of provision. Thus, just as government was beginning to consider modifying the school system, and just as employers were beginning to accept such changes, so the new tendency of Communist policy was to suggest that henceforth the path of socialist strategy was in the mere extension of rights which were already in part being gained. There was, certainly, much to be reformed. In the early 1930s, cuts in teachers' salaries, and in free places at secondary schools, were superimposed on the poverty of depression and defeat. This background of want inevitably placed the fight for the most basic levels of educational and material provision among the priorities of the labour movement, and of those outside it who supported reform. The problem for socialists was to support reform without accepting either its methods, which, entirely state-orientated, neglected to stimulate in the labour movement a discussion of the objectives of reform, or its limited horizons. The task of *critical* support was more important than ever, but was not carried out. 'English education is at the crossroads,' stated a CP publication in 1935, 'but we are free to choose which way we shall lead it; the way of Fascism . . . or the way of progress and a new society.'[34] Posed like this, the alternatives amounted to fascist reaction and a progress that was left undefined: was the 'way of progress' socialism or a reformed capitalism? From this ambiguous starting point, the CP, from 1935, supported a programme that was a set of demands for the expansion of education and of opportunity, including a class size of thirty, a leaving-age of 16, a massive rebuilding of schools, full welfare provision, and a 'brains test not a means test' for access to secondary education.[35] The last excepted, all were undoubtedly essential components of a policy for action. They did not, though, constitute a programme that could stimulate discussion on socialist educational objectives; the themes of the 1920s were not renewed.

Communists after 1944

In the years leading up to 1944, then, those who had previously
been responsible for the most substantial critique of education
adopted positions that responded to the prospect of expanded state
education in a one-sided, over-welcoming way. The new
institutions of schooling would be acclaimed as conquests of
democracy; the imperatives of economic modernisation rendered
indistinguishable from socialist educational aspirations. Such was
the response to the 1944 Education Act. G. C. T. Giles, President
of the NUT and a leading Communist teacher, posed himself two
questions about the Act: 'Does the Education Act give expression
to a modern, democratic outlook? Does it provide the framework
needed for a thorough recasting of our educational system?' The
answer was, 'Yes – on the whole, and in spite of certain
weaknesses, the Act is progressive and democratic. It does provide
a practicable working drawing for a new system.'[36] Such a position
could have been tenable had the Act really been the product of a
popular and radical campaign, and been a spur to further
mobilisation. In fact, as Quintin Hogg realised at the time, 'not the
least valuable feature [of the Act] is that it has placed the general
framework of our educational system beyond the range of party
politics'.[37] Commitment to an undefined 'modern' and
'democratic' outlook was not a sound enough basis on which to
build an alternative programme to that now ascendant. After 1944,
the communist policy tended to echo many of Labour's
assumptions. 'From where else [but the working class]', it asked in
1959, 'can we draw the large numbers of highly educated and
trained people we need if we are to survive as a great industrial
power? . . . The keynote of our policy is . . . the expansion of
educational opportunity at all levels.'[38] It is true that this approach
did not completely neglect issues of educational content. It was
pointed out that 'our children . . . are brought up to believe in the
essential justice of the existing social system, the basic unity of the
different classes'.[39] But this was usually mentioned in the context of
a general introductory discussion of the nature of schooling. When
it came to discussing the substance of a new policy, there was no
serious concern for matters of educational content; the relationship
between the school and the division of labour in society was not
seen as important.

It was not, of course, Communist militants who were responsible for the deradicalisation of educational debate. That responsibility was, rather, the Labour Party's. Nevertheless, their strategy did mean that no historic nucleus existed that could preserve older approaches and educate new militants. The Communist Party did work effectively in the NUT, despite heavy attacks upon it during the Cold War. In 1949, four out of its five members on the NUT Executive had lost their seats, following a scandal concocted from an apocryphal 'communist' circular to schools.[40] Later, as the Cold War became less intense, it regained some of its influence in the union, through its campaigns to defend living standards and achieve comprehensive reform. A mark of this influence was the election to the Executive, in the mid-1960s, of Max Morris, creator of an efficient progressive bloc among the union's activists. But this influence tended increasingly to be limited to the union apparatus. Morris was not in favour either of open campaigning for socialist policies, or of making radical critiques of education. Indeed, in the 1970s, he, alongside the Communist teachers' magazine, *Education Today and Tomorrow*, was a quite vitriolic critic of the 'new left' in education. It could not, by the 1960s, be said that anything remained, either among teachers, or among the labour movement as a whole, of important aspects of the traditions of the earlier part of the century.

A strong sense of professionalism

'Why has the NUT been so successful in dealing with the Communist problem?' asked Walter Roy, soon to be one of its executive members, in 1968. He suggested that the success arose:

> from the nature of [teachers'] work. School must place some emphasis on a code of morals, based on a concept of training children for citizenship in a democracy . . . There is a strong sense of professionalism among the teachers, thousands of whom labour in the schools, performing many unpaid tasks . . . who display a sense of vocation, a desire to impart to their pupils a quest for truth and objectivity.[41]

The years since 1968 have made plain the shortcomings of this argument. Nevertheless, it must have seemed at the time to be sound enough. The NUT had taken no significant industrial action for fifty years. The high-point of its commitment to reform had been reached in the war, when it had called for substantial experiments in comprehensive education.[42] Since then, it had passed into a slough of inaction from which it was only aroused by threats to its 'professional' status. When Durham County Council, in the early 1950s, had tried to impose a closed shop, 95 per cent of NUT members had threatened to strike. Walter Roy commented:

> More than ever before the teachers felt themselves to be members of a learned profession, whose sense of justice and decency had been outraged by the high-handed action of the county councillors, most of whom had no education beyond an elementary schooling.[43]

The activity of other unions provided no relief. Although verbally more militant, the NAS stunted even the most elementary conceptions of the unity of the workforce, through its continued attacks on the status of women teachers. Grammar-school teachers continued, on the whole, to be organised separately, men and women in different unions. Generally, men, despite the introduction in 1961 of equal pay, still held the dominant positions in teaching. A post-war increase of 40,000 male teachers, while women-teacher numbers remained static, had ensured that a new generation of headmasters and male union leaders could develop.[44]

Economically, teachers' conditions in the two post-war decades had worsened. There had been one abortive discussion of strike action, in 1961, followed in 1963 by government imposition of compulsory salary arbitration. The gains which could be registered strengthened teachers' professionalism, as well as their influence. Establishment of the Schools Council, alongside teacher-influenced CSE exam boards, made the NUT's dream of a self-governing profession tantalisingly close. If realised, this would have formed an alternative strategy to that of teacher trade unionism for defending working conditions and advancing teachers' interests.

It was reasonable, therefore, for Roy to describe teachers, in both educational and economic terms, as non-radical. He failed, though, to see the tendencies in both fields that would bring about change. In 1969, encouraged by the militancy of other unions, the

NUT and NAS went on strike over pay, and won £120 of a £135 claim. Shortly afterwards, in 1970, impelled by the success of the pay campaign, and anxious to gain access to discussions with the government about the place of education in its overall policy, the NUT affiliated to the TUC. (The NAS had done so shortly before.) Meanwhile, comprehensive reorganisation, a growth in teacher numbers and a continuing teacher shortage had created larger workplaces, wholescale curricular change, under the impetus of progressive ideas, and a more volatile teaching force. Some of the old divisions – between secondary-modern and grammar-school teachers, and male and female unions – began to break down. New hierarchies of status had not yet fully developed. New educational principles, new forms of control of the workforce, had still to be consolidated.

1968 and after – active trade unionism

The result was a period – from 1968 to 1974 – of some tumult, against a national background of industrial and political unrest. This was the formative period of a new, minority current in education. Unlike the traditional movements for equal opportunity, this current was inclined to see the school as a repressive institution; in contrast to traditional teacher unionism, it was eager to adopt trade-union methods of struggle. It was sympathetic to school-student movements and anxious to stress the potential radicalism of classroom activity.

It enjoyed advantages that were unavailable to earlier movements. Unlike the TLL, it came to life not at the close of a time of struggle, but at its blissful dawn. Rather than being hemmed in by surveillance and victimisation, it had, licensed by official curricular reform, a larger classroom space in which to operate. Instead of existing as a tight, beleaguered and isolated opposition, it had the unstructured energy, the spontaneous growth, the diffused and pervasive influence of a movement with real, if limited, social roots.

The new movement, from its beginnings, had two distinct, if overlapping, components. The first was militant trade unionism, expressed at first through the 'Rank and File' organisation; the second, less organised but more diffuse, was a curricular radicalism.

Rank and File

Our work continually involves compromise of our principles in so far as we are required to prepare pupils for examinations and tests which are anti-educational; to exercise an authority and control over children which we may frequently disagree with; to coerce pupils into conformity when conformity means subservience to a host of social evils. We are paid to serve the interests of state rather than the interests of pupils.[45]

The contrast with the views of Dr Roy could not be sharper: a claim that the system is repressive and anti-educational; a questioning, not just of the quantity of education, but of its principles, linked to an impatience with a union 'which almost invariably refuses to take a militant stand on anything at all', and is run by 'headteachers and others with a vested interest in the status quo'.[46] With such statements, Rank and File aggressively intruded upon the stillness of union life and the relative harmony of educational debate. It was formed in 1967–8, out of a growing domestic teacher discontent with low pay, the turbulent working conditions of comprehensive reorganisation, and the continuing authoritarianism of most schools. Home-grown radicalism was intensified and given a broader ideology by the events of May 1968 in France, which were discussed extensively in early issues of *Rank and File* magazine.[47] The impetus then given by student activity to working-class struggle seemed to indicate that such groups as teachers were no longer to be confined to the periphery of struggle. The events also suggested the possibility of struggle not just on the economic level, but also in and over the institutions which served to reproduce 'bourgeois ideology', among them the school. The interpretation of the events made by teachers in England was that they were a struggle against hierarchy and for egalitarian participatory democracy. An early issue of *Rank and File* noted 'the brittleness of arrogant educational authorities before the assaults of determined radicalism'. It approved the mass participation which characterised the rebellion of 1968, and which promised 'a thoroughgoing democratisation of French society'. It drew the conclusion that:

> It should now be obvious for socialists that education must involve student and teacher participation in control of the running of all educational institutes . . . In future teachers should discuss with pupils and exchange ideas instead of merely reciting long-prepared lessons.[48]

This was a long way from a strategy of demanding the expansion of an education whose principles and procedures were unquestioned. It was an approach that had more success than any politically radical educational movement since the 1920s. In its heyday (1972–4) *Rank and File* had a print order of 10,000 copies[49] and a membership of over 1,000. In the unfortunate words of a pamphlet it issued in 1974, it 'quickly mopped up numbers of the new generation of teachers'.[50] It addressed itself to the new generation's concerns: pay, the hierarchy which dominated them and seemed to be the main obstacle to progress in the schools, and the undemocratic union structures, dominated by head-teachers. The three issues were seen as closely related:

> Rank and File is unique in putting forward a total integrated philosophy for education. The school's role as a microcosm of the hierarchical capitalist society we live in leads to an analysis of the changes we seek and the fight necessary to introduce them. The main pillars of this policy are: democracy in schools . . . a single salary scale for teachers to fit in with a democratic school structure, and real, not illusory democracy in the union.[51]

Of these pillars, the most important were those founded upon union activity. 'Democracy in schools', as we shall later show, did not inspire the detailed working-out of an educational policy.

Such a gap can only be explained by reference to the militant trade-union activity of 1969–74, and the way in which its political implications were interpreted by the left at that time. The strikes against trade-union legislation, the success of important wage claims, the militancy of picketing and factory occupations were the dominant and most magnetic features of those years. Rank and File achieved much at this time in placing unity with these struggles on the NUT agenda, as a near-legitimate issue. Locally – especially in London, before the union rules were changed to prevent autonomous action – it was able to organise strikes on May Day, and against the imprisoning of dockers under the Industrial Relations Act. On issues that directly affected teachers, there was similar success. In 1974, after the electoral fall of Edward Heath, and before the second election of that year allowed Labour to consolidate the policies of the Social Contract, came the period of the successful 'London Allowance' campaign, based on unofficial, mass strike action. This, by no means under Rank and File control, formed the mould in which Rank and File's later attitudes were cast. In 1973, *Rank and File* had given up its magazine format to become an 'agitational' newspaper. The assumption was that it was now possible, in a situation of considerable economic militancy, to reach thousands of newly active teachers. To talk to them about the immediate issue of action was more important than to engage in general debate about educational issues. The experience of the London Allowance strikes seemed to confirm this view, but were in reality a false dawn. The relatively large 'Houghton' pay award at the end of 1974, which introduced wide and divisive differentials, was one sign of night regathering. The introduction by the NUT Executive of 'Rule 8' against autonomous local action was another. But the reborn tradition of militant union politics was cast into darkness most of all by the condition of the trade-union movement as a whole: its inability to produce a political alternative, beyond sectoral militancy, that would serve as an answer to the policies of the Labour Cabinet and of the trade-union signatories of the Social Contract. Decline in industrial militancy, added to changes in the union, removed the conditions for the success of unofficial NUT militancy.

Problems of trade unionism

Rank and File's failure to come to terms with this new situation created severe problems. As the possibilities for militant unofficial action lessened, so the stress put upon it by Rank and File intensified. 'There is now no getting away from the fact that if our executive refuses to fight on our behalf, and the anger of teachers is deep and strong enough, members will take up the cudgels on their behalf, forcing a reluctant executive to act', wrote Chanie Rosenberg in 1975,[52] establishing a scenario for the next few years. The building of unofficial action became the centre of Rank and File strategy. In the context of the years after 1974, this was an orientation to what was, in any significant terms, near-impossible. It reduced the ability of Rank and File to influence large numbers of teachers, reinforced the tendency to neglect educational issues, and intensified strains within Rank and File itself. Within the union, Rank and File declined. By 1981 it had lost both the seats its members held on the National Executive. Sales of its magazine had fallen to about 2,000.[53] In the course of these years it had suffered splits – arising mainly from its emphasis on unofficial action – which led to the formation of another left organisation, the Socialist Teachers' Alliance. Likewise, the decline of its educational interests led to the growth of magazines such as *Teaching London Kids* and *Radical Education*, which saw a need to develop an educational policy.

In late 1982, as this chapter is written, the Socialist Workers' Party – whose members are dominant in Rank and File – is discussing whether or not to turn it into a body whose main function would be to act as a recruiting agency for the party among teachers. The parallels with the decline of the TLL are striking.

An assessment of the Left

It is here appropriate – before discussing radical tendencies which could be described as 'pedagogical' – to make some assessment of the TLL and of Rank and File, organisations that have tried to develop a politics of education in a wider sense. Although it will not frequently be possible to find in their activity a detailed elaboration of 'socialist pedagogy', they have taken up, even if sometimes only implicitly, broad and basic issues: the 'class position' of teachers; the relation of socialist to progressive education; the attitudes of Marxists to the mainstream educational ideas of the labour movement; alliances among teachers, and between teachers and others. They considered such issues in a practical, as well as in a theoretical, way. As a political tendency, for instance, the TLL could not afford to confine its work to the discussion and diffusion of ideas. Educational ideas had to be linked to the task of creating organisations. It was not that ideas were demoted to an entirely secondary role, but rather that they were enlisted and deployed in ideological battle, and valued more for their ability to serve as clear standard-bearers of opposition than for their subtlety as instruments of exploration. Some such process is a part of any political activity. It will be argued, however, that in the case of the TLL and, much more, of Rank and File, this process was not accompanied by an understanding of the political importance of the type of ideological work that could demolish opposing ideas and construct satisfactory alternatives to them. This weakness, along with some fairly blatant tactical and political failings, has harmed the intervention of each successive 'left'.

The major weaknesses have occurred in three areas. In the first place, the relationship between teachers and the working class – and the difference between teachers and other trade unionists – have not adequately been clarified. Second, precise analysis of the development of the education system has been lacking; and so, consequently, has the ability to encounter critically progressive educational thought and to develop alternatives to it. Last, there has been no sustained confrontation with the ideas of the major influence upon educational reform, the Labour Party; instead, a range of unsatisfactory positions, varying from utter disdain to substantial assimilation, has been adopted.

The TLL: teachers and workers

On what basis, and through what methods, was the alliance between teachers and working-class organisations to be constructed? The TLL was aware of the difficulties of the task, and of the distance that teachers put between themselves and their potential allies. Its links with the EWI put it in a position to understand that the distance would not be lessened through struggles for bread alone. The EWI attempted to deal with the specific oppression of teachers, as well as their common interests with other workers in the struggle for socialism:

> In this society, not only are teachers unable to be the bearers of a superior culture to youth, but themselves fall into an intellectual dependence on bourgeois society ... The liberation of

educational workers from their miserable position is, from the material as well as the intellectual point of view, linked with the liberation of the school from its subordination to capitalism and with its transformation into a true workshop of culture for the whole of humanity.[54]

Thus the EWI recognised – but did not develop – an argument that teachers were not simply 'part of the working class', but, rather, experienced specific, additional kinds of oppression to which socialists must be attentive. The TLL, however, did not develop these ideas. In depicting the relationship of teachers to the working class, it applied essentially economic explanations of teacher ideology and of the mechanisms by which it would change. Teachers were part of the labour aristocracy 'which will be undermined by the dry rot of the capitalist system'. They were 'but the best-paid section of manual labour' whose non-political attitudes, 'a Victorian survival', would be swept away by the crisis. Thus the 'paramount importance of hammering out an economic policy to form the basis of work in the professional organisations'.[55]

The consequences of such an approach for educational policy were plain. To assume that teachers would be forced to the left by their worsening economic circumstances was also to infer that the development of an educational programme was not, from the point of view of activity among teachers, a priority. Likewise, there was no great need for an analysis of the changes in the English educational system: to know the movement of the economy was to know all.

The TLL's educational policy

These conceptions did not prevent the TLL being alive to educational issues, but they meant that it tended more towards sporadic criticism and general declaration than to specific analysis. In the interests of polemic, the TLL reduced an understanding of a complex and changing system to a grasp of simple, invariant features: force, intellectual distortion, militarism. It attacked its most obnoxious and reactionary aspects: Empire Day, the political surveillance of teachers, the ardent anti-socialism of most history textbooks.[56] But however valuable as a peg for agitation, such an emphasis dealt only with (increasingly) incidental features of the school. The challenge to socialists really lay in developing a coherent attitude – supportive or critical, as necessary – to change and proposed change in education. But the TLL devoted little attention to evidence of change: the incorporation of aspects of progressive education within state policy, or the gradual growth of 'equal opportunity' through the expansion of the grammar school. The covers of *Educational Worker*, which depicted students as puppets, performing dogs or dummy-sucking babies under instruction from bemedalled generals, were less accidents of caricature than reflections of the substance of the League's approach.

Potentially, the TLL's acquaintance with Soviet education offered a vantage point from which to criticise progressive education. As Dewey realised, the Soviet school both developed the principles of progressive education and challenged them. The activity it encouraged extended beyond the classroom and was not associated with preparation for limited and fixed roles in the division of labour. Yet although in *Educational Worker* there was much propaganda for the Soviet system, there was no serious attempt to utilise its example in a critical study of English progressivism. This was partly because the League lacked a stable concept of polytechnic education. On some occasions it was presented as 'the linking up of education with the social life of the people';[57] on others, as a means by which 'boys and girls are trained to become effective industrial workers'.[58] Absent from either type of presentation was polytechnic education's potential to overcome the effects of a mental/manual division of labour on the work of the school.

Instead of such direct intellectual confrontation, the League's criticism of progressive education took three forms, all somewhat tangential to the main body of progressive thought. First, it attacked the politically explicit statements of the progressives, which were easy targets. Second, it drew attention to the privileged social context of many of their experiments. 'Some of us', commented a TLL visitor to a progressive independent school, 'felt that such grim and sordid problems as the class struggle were outside the ken of these comely, healthy denizens of a far-away beauty spot in Hampshire.'[59] Third, the League, while approving of progressive reform, argued that the government would not carry it out. When the Hadow Report was published, for instance, it would have been possible for the League to compare its limited conceptions of 'practical activity' with those of the Russians. Instead the line was one that combined approval of Hadow with warnings that the government would not spend the money to carry out its proposals: 'Hadow proposes, Percy [President of the Board] disposes.'[60] Neither separately nor together did these three approaches represent a sustained criticism or assessment of progressive education.

A drift into sectarianism

Similar problems undermined the TLL's ability to develop alternatives to ideas generated in the mainstream of the Labour Party. It certainly recognised the importance of countering views such as those of Tawney, and refused a narrowly teacher-based or sectoral approach; it saw itself contributing to revolutionary educational politics not just in the NUT but in the labour movement as a whole. From 1926, however, it faced two obstacles – its own expulsion and the political aftermath of the General Strike – which for any organisation would have been insuperable. The new situation that these developments created – in which, for instance, the building of 'Workers' Councils on Education' was not a serious possibility – faced the League with two realistic tasks. On the one hand, it could have established itself as the critical left wing of the reform movement, supporting particular measures of reform, campaigning for demands of a radically democratic kind, and criticising the caution of Labour. On the other hand, it had the task of carrying out the intellectual work necessary to develop alternatives to Labour's programme of equal opportunity.

Neither work was accomplished. The League tended to adopt 'ultimatist' solutions to problems of strategy, which found no means of constructing an alliance to fight for particular reforms, and which assigned no role to the fight for reforms in the struggle for socialism. 'The whole question of education', wrote its secretary in 1928, 'is bound up with the overthrow of capitalism.'[61] – a platitude unhelpful as a strategic instrument. The 'Third Period', of course, exacerbated such tendencies to a point where practical participation in movements for reform was ruled out as a form of class collaboration. The theory produced at this time tended towards a rigorously functional view of education: it was there to defend, slavishly and harshly, the established order. It allowed no space for debate or dissident activity, no room for serious reform. 'In the capitalist regime', declared the French section of the EWI in 1930, 'the instituteur is not and never will be, whatever his personal opinions, anything but an instrument in the hands of the bourgeoisie to subjugate the masses.'[62] Likewise, the TLL, which argued that the teacher, as a disciplinary agent of the bourgeoisie, was to be classed with the policeman and the soldier, rather than with the productive worker.[63] In the light of such arguments, a socialist practice in state education was seen to be virtually impossible, since it was precisely the (unchangeable) ideological work of teachers that linked them to the interests of the state. They would break from these interests only through participation in the political and economic struggles of the working class.

By 1930 the League, acting in accordance with these theories, had jettisoned much of its educational programme, and its aims had been redrafted to centre on 'real and practical' demands which 'show up the complete betrayal by the Labour Party of the interests of the working class'.[64] As has already been indicated, the real effect of this position was to liquidate much of the radical educational heritage of the 1920s. When, in the mid-1930s, Communist hostility towards Labour abated, the new Communist Party programme drew more from the ACE than from the TLL.

Rank and File: the militant solution

The TLL began its most active work at dusk, in the gloom created by the defeat of the General Strike. By contrast, Rank and File, forty years later, had the advantage that its origins coincided with a rise in industrial militancy, and with a growth in radical educational and social movements. Initially, as we have seen, it borrowed much from May 1968, in particular the conviction that it was possible to struggle successfully in the institutions that reproduced bourgeois ideology. But it was by industrial militancy that Rank and File was eventually most influenced. Its formative years were those of the first national teachers' strike, and of the struggles against Industrial Relations legislation, and in solidarity with the miners' strikes of 1972 and 1974.

These strikes, and the mass activity that accompanied them, were the most dominant features of those years. I remember marching, as a student, at the back of the TUC demonstration against the Industrial Relations Bill in 1971 and being overwhelmed simply by its size; it was clear that any socialist activity which sought influence would have to involve itself in that movement. Any other orientation seemed merely eccentric. But along with this unavoidable and heartening realisation went an underestimating of its limits; no one on the left could imagine that the power that had been let loose against Heath's government could be tamed by the return of . . . Harold Wilson. We anticipated continued mass strikes, a confrontation between the demands of the workers and the policies of Labour, leading in some expectations to the breaking of Labour's virtual monopoly over working-class politics, in others to splits in the Labour Party, in all cases to alterations in the landscape of the left. The driving force of such processes was to be the economic struggle. This was seen as *the* means by which workers (and, by extension, teachers) were going to reject the old ideas. The extent to which trade-union militancy was politically compatible with support for the policies of Labour was not imagined. It was inconceivable that the masses or, at least, their grassroots leaders would tolerate the Social Contract, would not see through Labour or force it to the left. A recognition of the strength of the trade unions, of the capacities of millions to organise, to show solidarity, to display hatred of the Tories, coincided with a tendency to think that these things were enough. Belief in parliamentary democracy, in the progressive nature of the Labour Party, in the beneficial character of state education, were all destined to obliteration in the firestorms of industrial militancy. The assumption was widely shared on the left, but it was particularly firmly held by the 'International Socialists' (later the Socialist Workers' Party), who were effectively the leadership of Rank and File.

Such a context of political belief meant that Rank and File's approach was in several senses less complete than that of the TLL. The League's programme, for all its problems, at first reflected the experience and debates not just of teachers, but of the working-class movement as a whole. The new radicalism's origins and concerns were more sectoral, its links with the trade-union movement founded on the ground not of politics but of wage militancy. The TLL was influenced by a native and thriving tradition of socialist educational activity and by an international debate which raised basic theoretical questions. It was assisted by the Soviet Union's efforts to establish, and to demonstrate to the world, a distinctively socialist education. This potential heritage was neither easily accessible nor sought after by Rank and File.

Not only, though, did Rank and File not learn from the experience of the 1920s. Far more crucially, it tended to neglect the experience of the four following decades. In particular, no attempt was made to interpret and reconsider 'equal opportunity' as a strategy, nor to appreciate the extent of its influence. Rank and File was unique on the left in not making it a cornerstone of policy. But, as a strategy, it was bypassed rather than confronted. Its functions were not understood: to suggest the goals that the whole labour movement should fight for, and to provide a motivating ideology for educational change that would be acceptable as the basis of an alliance extending beyond the labour movement. Few efforts were devoted to analysing 'equal opportunity' or to suggesting how alternatives to it could be constructed.

Rank and File thus paid little attention to some of the problems that had preoccupied the TLL. We have considered the unsatisfactory way in which the TLL dealt with relations between teachers and the working class as a whole. For Rank and File, this was a problem that scarcely arose. A common militancy was thought to be the unifying factor. That the central slogan of Rank and File's early years should have been 'Democracy in Schools' shows how little concern there was for helping to reshape the educational ideas of the labour movement as a whole. It was a sectoral slogan, the result of a radicalisation *within* education. It was a demand, essentially, for the liberation of the class teacher. It did not relate to the content of education, nor to its popular control. One of its assumptions, for instance, was that, within the democratic framework, class teachers 'will decide what methods they use'.[65] As a reaction to head-teacher despotism, this was understandable; as part of a programme intended to unite teachers with potential supporters outside the school, it was inadequate.

Similarly, Rank and File's attitude to educational ideologies was affected first by an unreflective closeness to progressive ideas, and later by a trade-union-accented sectionalism. In its early years, Rank and File breathed in a belief in progressive education, evident in its manifestos, from the radical air around it: 'Progressive teachers will link up with others in their schools to agitate for change on a variety of issues – such as the involvement of parents, support for pupils' organisations, the introduction of progressive ideas.'[66] Progressive education was accepted, undefined, and assumed to be synonymous with socialist change. The actual practice of progressivism was left unquestioned and undisturbed. When, in the mid-1970s, Rank and File became convinced that militant trade unionism was the essence of strategy, it became more critical of progressive education. 'Democracy in schools' was rejected, and progressive education treated with more suspicion. But the new criticism was based on a classically trade-union concern for working conditions, rather than on ideological grounds. One article condemned progressive education in primary schools by showing how it made teachers work harder, and provided only an illusion of collective decision-making.[67] Another writer[68] proposed as an alternative to 'democracy in schools', 'trade union control of the workplace' – a slogan devoid of reference to parental or student involvement. In the later 1970s, Rank and File, under the pressure of the 'Great Debate', recovered some interest in classroom activity – by producing, for instance, 'anti-racist' teaching packs[69] – but it cannot be said that this was related either to a systematic attempt to develop this aspect of strategy, or to a serious assessment of educational objective.

Corresponding to this weak way of dealing with progressive education was a lack of concern with the influence of the Labour Party. Whereas the TLL came to denounce it, ferociously, Rank and File tended to ignore it. Such neglect was an almost universal complaint of the left in the euphoric aftermath of 1968; it was less widespread, and pardonable, later. Articles on the Labour Party, or on equal opportunity, were few. No basis of analysis was laid from which the achievements and problems of reform could be understood. Instead, the school was subject less to discussion of change and function than to polemical assertion:

We believe that they [repressive education, teachers' working conditions] arise from the nature of the present educational system. This system, like the social order of which it is an inseparable part, is destructive of the individual personality of the child and serves the needs of a society divided by age, sex, race and above all by class . . . The system is emotionally repressive . . . It perpetuates the class divisions of society . . . It provides no escape for the working class child.[70]

This could have been written at any time in the last hundred years, and would not, at any time, have been untrue. But as an approach capable of identifying particular trends and points of change it was unproductive. Not surprisingly, the main changes of the 1970s, in particular the growth of the 'school to work' lobby and the response of the labour movement to it, have passed Rank and File by.

A break in the routine

It is difficult to see how a socialist educational tendency can successfully be established without attention being paid to the major strategies and ideologies of progressive education and of the labour movement, and without the most detailed concern for the changing demands made of education by the interests that affect it. It is plain that neither the TLL nor Rank and File managed to cope with such issues. Some of their shortcomings arose from the inherent difficulty of building a political tendency within education, given the importance of the major union, the NUT, in formulating policy and organising teachers. All the efforts needed to establish a credible presence in the union – the need to win support for resolutions, to co-ordinate activity, to organise union action – mean that the daily practical bias of work is away from consideration of general and complex issues. Professionalism, equal opportunity, progressive education are all issues that have been neglected in this way. The pressure of routine tends to force activists to treat the NUT as a 'union like all the others', and teachers, by extension, as just another sub-group of the species 'worker'.

But such pressures, if unavoidable, are not irresistible. The failures of socialist tendencies do not only result from a succumbing to routine. It is also necessary to speak of an antipathy towards the work of developing analysis and strategy. Militant trade unionism has not simply been a dominant area of interest; it has been, also, illegitimately utilised to 'solve' or evade problems of strategy in areas as diverse as opposition to progressive education and the construction of alternatives to Labour's programme. To these weaknesses must be added those of a trade-union practice which frequently declined into sectarianism and grossly misread the 'balance of forces'. The result of such efforts has been not just an ineffective challenge to the hegemony of particular strategies, but the squandering of possible legacies from which alternatives to these strategies could be in part constructed.

From the negative experience of these tendencies we can draw two further conclusions. The first is that the changes in 'teacher consciousness' that left tendencies have hoped for will not come about unless teachers in large numbers question the principles of the work they do. Trade-union struggle may help prepare the conditions for such a questioning – but cannot substitute for the educational dimension of activity in posing the questions themselves. Likewise, we can conclude that alliances – with an educational content – between teachers and other sections of the working population will not be constructed on a 'unilateral' basis, through the movement of teachers towards trade-union forms of struggle. Rather, alliances will be based on a dual movement, whose second aspect will be the development, by forces outside teaching, of 'independent' popular objectives in education. On both counts, therefore, it is crucial to explore some of the areas that the TLL and Rank and File indicated, but into which they did not venture.

Curricular socialists

To have discussed these organisations is not, of course, to have exhausted the treatment of socialist activity in state education. It is important also to make some assessment of the curriculum-orientated work of socialists, particularly over the last fifteen years. This work is distinguished from earlier radical phases of pedagogy both by its extent and by its more explicit relationship to political objectives. To rephrase Neill's remark, the East End *is* a political problem, and the school can help elucidate it.

One of the earlier consequences of Rank and File's educational weaknesses had been a justified discontent among radical teachers at its increasingly narrow focus on issues appropriate to trade-union debate. However, discontent did not generate a complete alternative. There was always a tendency for educational issues to be considered not so much at the level of general policy, but rather in terms of their implications for the classroom.

This has tended to be the case with *Teaching London Kids*, the longest-lived of radical educational publications. *TLK*'s emphasis has been on what it is possible for teachers to achieve, in their individual classrooms and departments, or at the level of school policy. In this area, its achievements have been impressive: a stress on developing the critical response of working-class children to their social situation; an ability to connect debates on large issues – such as assessment – to an interpretation of classroom practice that shows the incompatibility of reactionary educational ideas with broadly 'progressive' social attitudes. Chris Searle describes the achievement as:

> the growth of a new methodology and classroom consciousness of working-class students themselves using their own local resources, perceiving their own neighbourhood, families, histories and themselves – in short, their class – as relevant and proper material to form a basis of knowledge and identity.[71]

Although there are here evident continuities with the perspectives of a Halsey, there are also important differences. The 'problems' of working-class education are seen as 'soluble' only by an approach that encourages the realisation in the classroom of collective, though often unspecified, 'working-class values'; this is accompanied by a willingness to introduce specifically political attitudes into the classroom.

Alongside the development of such a methodology, the magazine has suggested a political strategy – described by one of its editors in 1980 as 'capturing the middle ground'.[72] This strategy has entailed an attempt to demonstrate the effect of major developments in educational politics upon classroom practice. The intention has been to persuade teachers that, if they wish to defend their present methods of teaching, they will need to take a more consciously political stand. Conservative financial and ideological attacks, teacher professionalism, the continuing influence of church schools, have all been dealt with from this viewpoint.[73] In its willingness to politicise the classroom, and its conception that a political strategy is necessary to defend progressive gains, *TLK* is in advance of customary progressivism. Nevertheless, there are weaknesses. Discussion of strategic issues has been carried out in an incomplete and allusive way, which has taken for granted the strengths of progressivism. In the face of present attacks it has been assumed that the best response is not so much a re-examination of practice and strategy as a defence of what has already been achieved: 'Teachers should explain better their achievements and discuss more with parents, school students and managers, as a way of fighting potential isolation.'[74] This seems to reduce the problems of isolation to those of publicity and dialogue; it suggests that progressive education, whether in the classroom or in its relation to broader objectives, is unproblematic. In its efforts to present radical work in a positive, utilisable way, *TLK* avoids not only the snares of abstraction but also the necessary work of confronting the various premises of progressive education, and of beginning to elaborate an alternative to its methods, inside and outside the classroom. (In this fault, of course, it has the companionship of many others.)

Warrenism

One sign of this failure has been the tendency for *TLK* to graft its close attention to classroom practice on to political perspectives imported *en bloc* from elsewhere: Rank and File's trade-union politics in the early issues; a programme of anti-Tory egalitarianism later on. Such a rough-and-ready combining of disparate practices in order to cope with the difficulties of a situation that required an all-round perspective of some complexity indicates a considerable weakness – product not of the inadequacy of editorial collectives but of the entire method of radical-progressive advance. E. P. Thompson has written of the English working class after the defeat of the Chartists that, 'having failed to overthrow capitalist society, [it] proceeded to warren it from end to end'.[75] The warrens comprised those self-organised class institutions constructed after 1848: trade unions, co-operatives and so on. The metaphor is a suggestive one. It implies a withdrawal from central confrontation and 'global' perspective to sectoral initiative and local outlook. As such, it has a certain relevance to the radical educational practice of the last fifteen years. Teachers were presented with the field opened up by the officially promoted curriculum development of the 1960s, a field that was eagerly entered and undermined in a hundred ways, from as many directions, by loosely associated bands of delvers. A respectable theme would be taken up and radicalised; 'relevance' would be given a social-political meaning; equal opportunity for girls would be translated as anti-sexism. Existing warrens were deepened, new ones begun.

These activities have had an uncertain relationship to official policy. Official harassment has not been severe. Influence in individual schools is sometimes hard to gain, but nearly always possible. The official incorporation of radical ideas has been as likely a response as their attempted repression. No written sanction, no Schools Council justification exists for many of these activities; but nor are they forbidden. They are embedded in schools, protected by a tradition of teacher autonomy. However, the form of their development has limited their present scope. Their relative freedom to develop at classroom level has bred a certain limitation of vision; general questions, either of educational content or of strategy, have not been faced.

The most significant blindspot in the warren's field of vision has been that of 'education for industry'. This theme has inspired a sharp change in state educational policy, and has also instigated a criticism of the curriculum which has found a sympathetic response among those outside education whom teachers would regard as potential allies. Its virtual absence from radical thought means not only that 'anti-progressive' forces have gained a tactical initiative, but also that the left has great difficulty at present in dealing with issues of quite fundamental importance to a socialist conception of education. These issues only in part concern 'vocational' or 'prevocational' training. They relate also to the understanding created both of the technical process of production and of the relations between the classes involved in the labour process. It thus, in this latter respect, relates to the presentation of the whole social structure. Without some understanding of these relationships, it is difficult to understand the position and possibilities of the working class in any but a restricted way.

Outside the warren

Thus, radical interest in a 'working-class content' to education has been so far concerned largely with the class's 'autonomous' cultural and social existence. The class that is the focus of radical educational activity is not one that is seen in the context of its role in production, nor in relation to other classes in society. As the comments of Chris Searle indicate, it is seen as a community, but as a rather self-enclosed one, without a perspective on the rest of society. By contrast, previous Marxist educators have seen their purpose as helping to create just such a 'universal' perspective. Gramsci's argument, in discussing the difference between trade-unionist and political consciousness is valuable:

> Trade unionism stands revealed as nothing other than a form of capitalist society, not as a potential successor to that society. It organises workers, not as producers, but as wage earners . . . The worker can see himself as a producer only if he sees himself as an inseparable part of the whole labour system which is concentrated in the object being manufactured, and only if he experiences the unity of the industrial process . . . The worker will see himself as a producer if . . . he can . . . comprehend the whole of the Turin car-manufacturing process, if he can comprehend Turin as one large production unit characterised by the car; see a large part of the general productive activity of Turin as existing and developing simply as a result of the existence and development of the car industry . . . Starting off from this particular cell, the factory, seen as a unit, as an act that creates a particular product, the worker proceeds to the comprehension of ever vaster units, right up to the level of the nation itself . . . At this point the worker has become a producer, for he has acquired an awareness of his role in the process of production . . . At this point aware of his class.[76]

This approach illuminates a vantage point from which the themes of 'education for industry' – which offer only the most limited and immediate understanding of production – can be criticised without recourse to an anti-industrial and somewhat Luddite perspective. The direction of Gramsci's argument, however, would be unfamiliar to most radical teachers. In place of the analytic basis he suggests is essential to the formation of a 'universalist' consciousness, the stress of radical progressive education tends to be affective: 'Personal' writing, the communication of experience, predominates. It is true that the stress of such writing is no longer encouraged to fall on 'crises of everyday life' which 'have nothing to do with class'.[77] But its predominance, along with the continuing dominance of English in the curriculum, are signs of the limits of radicalisation. For on the map of radical education, English retains its central position. Of course, the subject 'English' has been much modified; its boundaries have been stretched by the attempt to encompass social and political issues. But a frontier remains. Although English can incorporate some issues, it remains extremely difficult, within the constraints of the usual pattern of the curriculum, of the exam system and of political prohibition, to pursue the kind of studies to which Gramsci alluded. Even though English departments are more likely than most to be staffed by radicals, English is a very unsuitable vehicle for a project like Gramsci's. While its traditions are more critical than those of other subjects, they are those of an anti-industrial culture-criticism, whose central concept of 'experience' does not address the structures of social life. By an irony that arises from the depths of English culture, the subject most disposed towards social criticism is one of those least capable of achieving the all-round understanding that Gramsci's programme necessitates.

The material uncovered even by this brief enquiry into the traditions that the left has at its back is cause for sobriety rather than for celebration. Although posing several crucial questions of political strategy and intellectual standpoint, it cannot be said to provide even remotely confident answers to them. Nevertheless, from the history of 'left' activities some important issues of political strategy and organisation and of educational philosophy and method emerge. It is upon these issues that the next, final chapter is centred.

6

Beyond progressive education

> The new conception of education will not proceed from the basic structures of the existing division of labour, christened 'demands of society'.[1]

Today the state educational system finds itself under-resourced and vulnerable to reactionary change. The possibility of even a modest development of equal opportunity is slight. The channels of influence painstakingly constructed by progressives are silting up.

The labour movement's answer to this situation is in essence a reprise of older positions, more radical in its attack on privilege, bolder in its approach to problems of post-16 education, but offering as little hope of popular mobilisation as ever, and nowhere showing awareness of connections between an intellectually impoverished education system and the necessities of political and economic life which keep it in that state. A Labour educational policy can only be radical if it is willing to address the dissatisfactions of those it claims to represent and if it comprehends the basis of that dissatisfaction in the division of labour for which the school prepares its successive generations. Labour's proposals are full of familiar and just criticisms of the cultural and technical backwardnesses of a segregated system of schooling, yet lack a rationale other than that which assumes that modernisation and democratisation are two sides of the same coin, and fail to criticise the restricted intellectual formation that the school develops.

To achieve a basis firm enough to sustain the development of a socialist education policy requires both a transcendence of

Labour's policies, and an extension of the left's current concerns. It entails more than the winning of battles against the cuts, more than the making political of a union, more than a radicalisation of the classroom. Such victories would be welcome, but partial and inconclusive. They would not in themselves be sufficient to transform progressive and 'labourist' conceptions of educational purpose.

How strong are the Conservatives?

It is from such a dissatisfied viewpoint that this chapter observes the present impasse of strategy and suggests means by which some roads out can be opened. These suggestions cannot be made without reference to the relationship of forces within which they could be worked out and applied. This entails, in turn, a calculation of the effects on education of Conservative policy, recession and social crisis. How strong are the Conservatives and how weak are their opponents? What are the extent and lasting effect of the changes brought about by Carlisle and Keith Joseph? Have they influenced popular educational ideas? In the aftermath of the 'Great Debate' and in the midst of education cuts, does the response of teachers have a conservative or a radical character?

The first parliamentary act of Mrs Thatcher's government was to repeal legislation designed to make comprehensive education universal. Since then, there has been a spate of laws, directives and initiatives on education: the Assisted Places Scheme; the introduction of 'parental choice'; the retreat from a common exam at 16; the MSC's 'New Training Initiative'; the abolition of the Schools Council. The list is formidable but, even so, does not represent the fulfilment of Conservative ambitions. Before the 1979 election, Conservatives dreamt of a mass movement of educational reaction. The Black Papers detected the emergence of a movement for 'parental rights' which they would champion against educational bureaucracy and classroom leftism. Rhodes Boyson spoke of a nationally imposed curriculum, and Conservative pre-election statements called for a national system of testing. The message was one of strong centralised intervention, backed by demagogic popular campaigns and by the recreation of 'market' pressures upon education.

The gap between intention and result remains wide. There have been changes that strengthen long-term conservatising pressures and demolish particular strongpoints of reform. Yet it is not possible to say either that conservative populism has become the dominant educational ideology, or that changes of a fundamental kind in educational financing and curricula have occurred. There has been an effective intervention in the area of educational policy-making, where there have been a number of measures taken to increase central control and limit the autonomy of the 'educational apparatus'. The replacement of the Schools Council by nominated rather than representative bodies on exam reform and curriculum return to the DES the initiative that it lost in the early 1960s, and lessen the influence of teachers and educationalists. The growth of the MSC, whose ten members include only one who represents 'professional educational interests', and which is responsible to the Department of Employment, is further evidence of a centralising tendency.

Even in this area, however, success has not been sweeping. Government guidelines on the school curriculum, which echoed some earlier calls for a return to basics, had to be heavily modified in response to educational criticism. Proposals for a national system of testing have failed to get off the ground. The Assisted Places Scheme is opposed by almost every educational interest, and is undersubscribed.[2] In short, the combination of curriculum reform and parental pressure has failed to materialise as a potent force.

Likewise, it has not achieved complete success in its efforts to restrict local government spending on education. The abandoning of sections of Heseltine's 'Local Government Bill' in 1981, and of plans to penalise heavily 'overspending' councils in 1982 are measures of the effectiveness of a defensive action carried out by local councils, in a context of popular campaigning against the most dramatic plans for local cuts. This, rather than any Boysonian programme, was the basis of parental mobilisation in Conservative Merton and Solihull in 1981.

It cannot be said, then, that the future direction of education has been settled. Much depends on the success of the Conservatives' overall political strategy. If they achieve a second term in office, if the attack on working-class living standards and achievements can be sustained over a long period, then the constraints on a proudly inegalitarian educational policy will have been largely removed. It would then be correct to anticipate considerable privatisation of ancillary services (meals, cleaning), the utilisation of falling rolls to increase greatly the rate of school closure and job loss, and the introduction of the 'market' principle into state education, through the use of educational 'vouchers'.[3] These would allow parents the 'choice' of 'buying' for their children education in the state or (for an additional sum) the private sector. Their use would allow – indeed force – popular schools to select which children to admit, and would create, alongside individual choice, great collective inequalities.

Tories and training

When the Conservatives came to office in 1979, it was upon these kinds of issue that their attention was focused. In office, priorities have changed. The major educational reorganisation, and the major concretisation of new priorities, is to be found outside statutory schooling, in the expansion of '16 to 19' education and training. The Government has been able to utilise the weakness of the ideas of educational reform in this area to establish, without significant contention, a pattern of education that embodies both a selective principle and a utilitarian interpretation of the purpose of mass education. If present proposals for the vast expansion of post-16 education, accompanied by the codification of 'pre-vocational' conceptions of mass education at this level, are implemented, then they will have a considerable effect on the character of schooling as a whole. As its final stage, they will cast the shadow of their priorities back on to the system as a whole. Regardless of the character of the governing party, educational policy in the 1980s will centre on the post-16 sector, and it is from there that the impetus to remodel large sections of education will come. It is therefore important to describe and comment upon what is proposed.

The initiative in expanding this sector has – symptomatically – been taken not by the DES, but by the Department of Employment. Norman Tebbit's original proposals, made in 1981, for youth training were widely criticised for their element of compulsion – unemployed youth who refused places on training courses would no longer qualify for state benefit – and for the suggested 'wage' of £15 a week. There was criticism of these (contingent) features, but little of the essence of the proposals, which were taken up and revised in the MSC's Youth Training Scheme.[4] At the same time, the DES announced a new 17 + 'pre-vocational' qualification, to be offered by schools and colleges.

The '17 + ' will, from September 1984, involve about 80,000 students. The Youth Training Scheme will by September 1983 involve 460,000 16- and 17-year-olds – about 25 per cent of the age-group – and will grow to involve even more. Together the projects form the biggest attempt to renovate English education since the mid-1960s. Neither scheme rests on a purely vocational conception of education, if by that is understood preparation for a particular, fixed job. Under the MSC's scheme every school-leaver would be entitled to training, usually lasting a year. Most training would be workplace-based, but there would be a minimum of three months' 'off the job' training and/or 'relevant' general education. Training would not consist only of the acquisition of the practical skills entailed in a particular job, but also of an 'introductory programme of training and skills related to a broad group or family of related occupations'.[5] This would be accompanied by education in good working habits, 'working to deadlines, sharing responsibilities . . . health and safety and work, role of trade unions, etc'.[6]

The 17 + school- and college-based courses offer a similar approach, developing practical skills, but also containing 'a broad programme of general education with emphasis on various types of employment'.[7] They, too, would aim to 'develop personal attitudes such as self-motivation, adaptability, self-reliance'.[8] It is always stressed that the purpose of such an education should not be defined in specific vocational terms; rather, it contributes towards the development of attitudes useful in the transition from school to work. Most discussion on the subject recognises that, in this respect, the new schemes have consequences lower down the secondary school. The 14–16 curriculum must develop 'the personal skills and qualities as well as the knowledge needed for working life'.[9] Overall, what is being established is a new educational ethos, arising from the requirements of the transition from school to work, but extending downwards from the post-16 curriculum to permeate and modify the traditional concerns of English secondary education.

It is in this area that Conservative policy is making the greatest immediate headway, largely as a result of its continuity with the type of approach outlined in the 'Great Debate'. But the consensual Youth Training Scheme is developing alongside an explicitly Conservative approach to other features of post-16 education. Although pre-vocational mass education will be expanded, the 'traditional' sixth form will be maintained. Sir Keith Joseph has in several cases, most notably Manchester's, turned down proposals for a tertiary organisation which would have meant the abolition of school-based sixth forms. The effect of such a position, combined with the pre-vocational character of new 16-plus training, creates the danger of a two-tier system, not resting on the comprehensive principle.

Labour's response

The response to the Youth Training Scheme of the TUC, the Labour Party and the NUT has, on the whole, been a welcoming one. The TUC objected to Tebbit's original proposals, but is happier with the non-compulsory revised version, which allows some trade-union monitoring of courses, and which promises a more stringent approach to the use of young people as cheap labour by employers who are supposed to be offering them training – one of the unions' chief complaints about the Youth Opportunities Programme, which preceded the YTS. The Labour Party considers the expansion of post-16 education as its educational priority. It has drawn attention to the possible dangers of a two-tier system, but expressed no great disagreement with the new system. Likewise the NUT, whose main worry has been the exclusion of schools from the development of the YTS.

Nowhere has there been fundamental criticism of the education proposed for the mass of the age-group. This weakness will have repercussions for the ability of the labour movement to define goals for the whole education system that are any different in kind from those expressed in and since the 'Great Debate'.

Defending equal opportunity – the Barking strike

If, in this crucial area, the response to Conservative initiative has been feeble, it has elsewhere been more robust. This has most notably been the case with the defence of existing educational provision. It is here that 'equal opportunity' has demonstrated its residual strength. It remains a limited but deep-rooted popular ideology. I have had vivid proof of its endurance in the NUT's seven-week strike, in 1982, against cuts in the London (Labour) Borough of Barking and Dagenham. The strike – the NUT's longest since the 1920s – was called to stop a proposed cut of 160 jobs, over 10 per cent of the teaching force. It was notable not just for its manifestation of teacher militancy, but for its popular character. The NUT, representing about 60 per cent of teachers, and not supported by other teaching unions, was able first to mobilise and then to work alongside newly created organisations of parents. Meetings between teachers and parents were held in half the borough's schools. An inaugural meeting of a 'Parents' Action Committee' attracted three to four hundred people. Parents organised regular occupations of the Town Hall, as well as demonstrations of several thousand parents and teachers in Barking and in London. Students at one comprehensive circulated others, urging them to support a demonstration. Fred Jarvis walked at the head of it, phalanxed, to his surprise, in a mass of students on their bikes. NUT members, for their part, distributed over a quarter of a million leaflets and collected within a week 15,000 signatures supporting their strike.

This is not to say that parents were unanimous in their support. The borough is dominated by large council estates, broken up by pockets of private housing. On these private estates, responses to the teachers tended to be less sympathetic. At one school, parents blockaded a bus taking teachers to a demonstration. At another, they applauded a speaker – the owner of a local sports shop – who denounced the teachers whose strike had made their children 'political pawns'. But, overall, this attitude had little resonance. A go-back-to-work movement collapsed almost as soon as it had begun. Most of the activity of parents was in support of the strike. Sustaining the struggle were the desire to defend quite basic levels of provision, an immense irritation with a council that showed scant interest in any educational matter, and a commitment to what was expressed as 'the future of the children'.

The 'lessons' that can be drawn from this experience confound those who see working-class commitment to education as eroded to the point of near eradication. They indicate, too, that there need be no contradiction between militant forms of industrial action, and the achieving of popular support. It might have been thought that the strike would have evoked a disapproving response that stressed the teachers' traditional, 'non-political' role, and that saw their primary and inescapable duty as the day-to-day care of children, no matter what problems were approaching over the horizon. But such criticisms, though components of the response to the strike, were never dominant.

Problems unresolved

The action in Barking and Dagenham demonstrated that cuts can be fought, and that those who fight them need not be isolated – provided that they emphasise not simply the sectional aspect of their aims (defence of jobs) but the wider implications of their struggle (defence of education). Yet, from a point of view that seeks to develop an overall socialist strategy, its success – nearly two-thirds of the jobs were won back – throws into relief the weakness of responses to other important changes in education. Defence of education as it existed – rather than the nature of the education that was being so fiercely defended – was the exclusive theme of the campaign. It demonstrated that there is no popular assent to measures designed to lessen educational opportunity through blatant reductions in provision. Even those hostile to the strike opposed the cuts. It does not, though, follow from this that other features of educational reform – curriculum, selection, educational method – are likely to give rise to militant defensive movements. For that to occur, even in modest form, there has to be some agency to shape popular demand, and at the same time to respond convincingly to its doubts and criticisms. But not one of the bodies that profess to uphold educational advance has sought to develop the kind of energies revealed, for instance, in the strike, in the direction of discussing a content to education, nor even of actively supporting the measures of reform that are proposed. A large part of the Labour Party is ill-disposed to such a task. 'Do you expect us to go on the knocker?' said one councillor in Dagenham when parents asked him why his party had done nothing to campaign against education cuts. And what is embodied in Labour's practice is codified in its theory. As the authors of *Unpopular Education* show, nothing in the speeches of the Shadow Education Secretary, Neil Kinnock, suggests a departure from an old pattern of policy development: policy is determined and implemented by experts. The 'people' intervene only for one brief moment, as electors. Little has been done to think out, let alone practise, new kinds of relationship between education and those whose interests it is supposed to serve.[10]

Polarising teachers – the NUT

If the strike indicated something of the popular resistance that the more palpable forms of reaction provoke, it also illustrated some recent developments among teachers. The threat of unemployment maintains one kind of discipline upon teachers; it is no longer a plausible response to react to pressure and job dissatisfaction with the threat of resignation. The Friday staffroom ritual of reading the job adverts in the *TES* now scarcely serves a useful purpose. Yet the result is not an entirely cowed 'profession'. Certainly, the cuts and the hard educational times have produced sharp polarisations among teachers. One aspect of the polarisation is, on the part of some, a rejection of any form of resistance. But, in the NUT at least, the years since 1975 have seen an increase in local militancy and a greater readiness to use trade-union forms of struggle. These developments have a significance for teachers' consciousness of their general social and political role. Increasingly, teachers have become willing to organise public activity which – a generation ago – they would have condemned as 'unprofessional'. During the Barking and Dagenham strikes, for instance, official NUT picket lines appeared, for the first time, outside comprehensive and primary schools. Unionised oil-tanker drivers refused to cross them. The council, in response, employed scab drivers. Teachers lay down in front of them, followed them to their depots, publicised the council's tactics. A council driver refused to cross the picket lines and was suspended. In their resulting strike, the council drivers were almost fully sustained by donations from the NUT members. Such action not only signified the (partial) acceptance of the union by the rest of the trade-union movement, but also an irrevocable local breakdown of the idea that the teacher's vocation and status rest on aloof disinterest in all matters – such as picketing – that are flashpoints of public controversy.

These remarks lead us to a more general consideration of the state of teacher trade unionism. The NUT, over the last decade, has moved closer to the frontline of educational reform, and to the issues that preoccupy the rest of the trade-union movement. In favour of 'universal' comprehensivisation, opposed to public schools, willing to defend (though not endorse) mixed-ability teaching, the union now also attempts to relate education to issues arising from social crisis, calling for 'schools to adopt a clear anti-racist stance [and] a school policy for tackling racism'.[11] Likewise, it is now capable of noting, at its 1982 Conference, 'that women teachers face a double threat from the present cuts – not only through loss of jobs but also through loss of services such as nurseries – as the government attempts to substitute unpaid domestic labour by women for social provision through the welfare state'. It recognises 'that women teachers suffer from the stereotype of women as the "natural" performers of domestic and child-care duties', and opposes 'sexual stereotyping' in the curriculum.[12] Yet, in all of these advances, there are weaknesses and hesitations – particularly where political issues 'intrude' into educational debate. Especially at leadership level, the union continues in its reluctance to endorse ideas and actions – such as campaigns against the trade-union legislation of the present government – that are common currency in other trade unions. Above all, it attempts to stay clear of overtly political issues. The sharpest political debate that the union has known since the 1920s occurred in its 1982 Conference over one such issue – unilateral nuclear disarmament. Against executive advice and presidential ruling, the Conference narrowly supported a resolution that aligned the union with campaigns against Cruise and Trident missiles and for unilateralism. The debate continued after the resolution. The union president, Alf Budd, announced that the union rules did not allow the resolution to be implemented, sought legal advice to confirm his position, and appealed, over the head of the Conference, to the rank-and-file members of the union to support him.[13] The union executive likewise refused to implement the resolution, thus setting the scene for prolonged contestation over the union's very identity.

The debate and its aftermath illuminated the union's basic dilemmas. Its traditional strategy, confidently resting upon the union having the great majority of teachers among its members, had been one of seeking to influence, as a pressure group, the policy of local and national administrations. Its positions on the Schools Council were perhaps the crowning achievement of this strategy. The development of the MSC, the breakdown of educational consensus, the changes in educational administration and the sharpness of the cuts all reduced the effectiveness of a 'pressure group' approach, and the union has to look around for other means of influence. This would seem to necessitate a closer alliance with other trade unions, a willingness to relate educational problems to solutions at the level of the economy, a campaigning rather than an 'expert' role in relation to public opinion, and an encouraging of action by its members to defend educational provision. The union has taken some steps down this road, and there is an increasingly strong, though not majority, influence which wishes to see it make further progress. But, at leadership level, there is no intention to arrive at radical destinations. Such a route would endanger the entire way in which the union has constructed its identity: that it represents, potentially, all teachers, and that to use the collective strength of the union to pursue non-educational or political ends would be to abandon such a role. To adopt a different strategy, it is argued, would mean, in the context of a polarising profession, a further loss in membership; already the union's share of the total teaching force has fallen below 50 per cent.

Thus the NUT, while by no means a beaten union, is, in strategic terms, stranded: exiled from the counsels of government, it has yet to find a new home.

Other teaching unions

What of the other teachers' organisations? The National Association of Schoolmasters/Union of Women Teachers (NAS/UWT), Assistant Masters and Mistresses Association

(AMMA), the Professional Association of Teachers (PAT) and the two heads' associations, NAHT and SHA, are together probably of comparable size to the NUT. Their relative growth over the last two decades can be ascribed to the new problems that teachers have had to face, and to the different political answers that have been offered to these problems. All, whatever the nuances of their response, are characterised by a defence of a 'traditional' and sectoral approach to a crisis of strategy. This approach comprises: opposition to cuts and to increasing central control of education; upholding of 'professional' standards against both political 'interference' and, in most cases, militant trade unionism; a tendency to adopt conservative positions on the school's role at a time of social crisis.

The PAT, founded in 1969 as a direct response to the NUT's rediscovery of militant action, has as its *raison d'être* a principled opposition to militant action. Its new chairman expresses its view with great clarity:

> Teachers who support industrial action are not only impudent, but also defraud parents by not providing education of the highest standards [and] defraud pupils by failing to provide proper care, leadership and good example . . . They are a small minority and the teaching profession would be better off without them.[14]

Similar, though less drastic, views flourish in the NAHT, whose 1982 President lamented new approaches to teachers' conditions of service, based on a trade-union interpretation of the working day: 'There are a growing number of teachers who hold a much narrower view of the duties that are required of them. Such teachers introduce an unhappy atmosphere of militancy into the school.'[15] These organisations, like the AMMA, see the teacher as someone capable of adhering to 'professional' standards of behaviour and competence, in no need of control by a centralised administration, and disdaining trade-union forms of action as the negation of professional responsibility.

The NAS/UWT is in some ways a different sort of organisation, especially in its willingness to organise industrial action to defend salary levels and working conditions. In the 1960s, it was able to use such credentials to win large numbers of male secondary teachers away from the NUT. In the 1980s, however, its militancy must be in doubt: its members have only once – in Trafford in 1980 – been permitted to take substantial action against cuts. Moreover, its bellicosity is very much related to the traditional concerns of teacher trade unionism: the defence of teacher autonomy. Despite its TUC membership, it has little interest in establishing any sort of unity of purpose with non-educational unions, and insists on its non-political nature. Unlike the NUT, this insistence is not subject to challenge from the union's own ranks.

Defence of 'autonomy', for the NAS/UWT, has a peculiar twist, deriving ultimately from the NAS's earlier emphasis on the school's inculcation of manly virtues – one of its slogans of the 1920s was 'men teachers for boys'.[16] 'Autonomy' includes the defence of the teachers' right to use corporal punishment, and it is on issues of this type that the union makes a distinctive contribution to educational debate. Whereas other associations distinguish themselves from the NUT in the distance they place between 'professional' and trade-union activity, the NAS/UWT combines an assertion that it is the most effectively militant trade union with a hue-and-cry about order in the classroom that frequently dovetails with the concerns of the Black Papers. In the early 1970s and, again, ten years later, the union has claimed to identify a rising tide of classroom violence, and has used this as justification for a campaign to strengthen 'discipline' in schools.

Such an attitude characterises the NAS/UWT's role in wider educational debate. When, for instance, at the 1980 NUT Conference two hundred delegates walked out during the address by the Secretary of State, several newspapers were able to contrast the NUT disorder with the blood-and-iron of the NAS/UWT Conference that was taking place at the same time. What the *Daily Express* called the 'shouting, heckling and banner-waving' at the NUT were counterposed to the rigour of NAS/UWT statements: 'Authority, discipline and morality have all come to be regarded with scorn.'[17] Similarly, when the NUT voted, in 1982, in support of unilateralism and, a couple of days later, against corporal punishment, the NAS/UWT was quick to declare its agnosticism on all political issues and its support for the corporal punisher.[18] Of course, it could be argued, these are the opportunist ploys of a membership war, rather than considered statements of belief. The important fact is, however, that they are statements whose existence is testimony to sharp ideological and political differences among teachers; they would not be made if it were not thought that they would find a welcoming response.

The NAS/UWT, then, is different from other non-NUT unions in the methods that it occasionally uses to defend its members' interests. But its horizons are no higher than theirs. It responds to a crisis of traditional strategy by a reassertion of sectoral interest, by manoeuvres to improve its bargaining position marginally at the expense of other unions, and by an opposition to new forms of 'interference'. It has nothing to offer that can overcome the impasse of strategy.

The sharpness of the divisions between and within the teaching unions indicates the impact that the changes in central educational policy are having upon them. It cannot be said that, out of these divisions and debates, a satisfactory response to the various aspects of crisis has yet emerged. When to these sectional problems is added the general weakness of the labour movement's educational policy, it can be seen that, although there will continue to be often active opposition to financial cutback and the more blatant forms of inequality, it is not the case that the most central features of educational restructuring will encounter criticism and resistance.

Beyond progressive education: among schoolteachers

It is appropriate that a book that claims to identify deficiencies in major educational traditions should itself conclude with an indication of the main lines of advance from the positions habitually adopted by those who have wished to defend and extend educational provision. Such a conclusion, although to an extent drawing upon existing practice, must in large part 'create itself'. From a reading of the weaknesses of the dominant strategies, and of those that briefly and tentatively, from the left, opposed them. I have tried to suggest those themes essential both to challenging a renascent reaction, and to establishing the beginnings of a practical alternative to the concerns that still preoccupy progressives and socialists. In the absence of a thriving debate on the issues, such suggestions must be provisional; although the conclusion of this book, they are merely prefatory to the real development of a socialist educational policy.

More than half a century ago, educational radicalism had its roots outside the state system, in the self-organisation of working-class movements and, remote from them, in the isolated experiments of some progressives. There has been no revival of such activity in the last decade. Instead, the origins of a new radicalism have lain within the state schools. Although it is impossible to speak of a contemporary movement as class-conscious as the Plebs League, there is compensation in the changes in the position of teachers, who are no longer almost homogeneously authoritarian, nor politically remote from the working class. A socialist strategy, thanks to the gains made by educational reform, has a greater opportunity than in the past to address itself to the prospects for a socialist strategy in the state sector.

Themes of a union strategy

I would argue that the main point of purchase of any attempt to gain support and initial momentum for such a strategy lies in the trade-union organisation of teachers – which, in the present context, means the NUT. No other locus suggests itself. For all its weaknesses, the NUT is the only major organisation that concerns itself with issues of educational content, attempts some popular campaigning, and adopts policies that can lead to militant action in defence of educational provision: the range of its activities extends beyond customary trade-union issues of jobs and working conditions. To concentrate efforts upon its further transformation is not, I would argue, an economistic idiosyncracy – provided that the concerns of socialists in the NUT are not restricted to the development of its industrial 'muscle'.

Three issues are important to the developing of a strong socialist current: the content of education, the winning of popular support, and the related tasks of accomplishing a further 'trade unionisation' of the NUT, while at the same time achieving a closer political relationship between the union and the labour movement as a whole. In each of these areas, a challenge to present attitudes is necessary.

As its response to the 'school and work' connection shows, the union's educational ideas are limited by its acceptance that occupational destiny should restrictively affect the content of courses. Alternatives to this argument will be suggested in the final section of the chapter. Here it is enough to draw attention not so much to the union's objectives, as to the methods that it advocates for educational advance. Like the other teaching unions, the NUT defends with vehemence the autonomy of the school in matters of curriculum and organisation. In practice, this entails a belief that such matters should be left to head-teachers, in consultation with their staffs. The assertion implies defence of the head's prerogative, in the last analysis, to resist pressures from the staff. While the NUT, like the NAS/UWT, will approve action of a trade-union kind – such as refusal to cover for absent staff – that challenges the head's customary powers, it has not extended the principle to the curriculum. Thus the educational activity of the union is not organised collectively, but is limited to the work of its representatives on such bodies as the Schools Council, examination boards, and LEA education committees. The union's educational policies are, of course, publicised among the membership, but they are intended to have a diffused influence, rather than to be formally adopted as objectives to be pursued in each school.

The teacher's separate lives, as professional and trade unionist, continue, thus, to be kept apart. The division could be narrowed if the NUT encouraged its members to press for union educational policy to be implemented through the activity of teachers in their schools. This would begin to make the routines of school life the subject of debate and contestation. Such a process would also entail the questioning of hierarchies within the school. During the 1960s, the aim of the employers was to increase salary differentials – a successful project which not only lessened salary costs but created new divisions and ranks of authority within the school. The teaching unions accept, in large part, these structures. They defend the existence of large pay differentials, and welcome heads, despite their managerial functions, into union membership, where they have an influence disproportionate to their numbers. As long as the NUT in these ways signals its acceptance of educational hierarchies, it will be difficult to develop radical policies at school level.

Teachers and popular control

A similar acceptance of educationally conservative ideas hinders any efforts the union may make to win popular support for educational reform. As an educational lobby it has always prized its ability to influence policy through a combination of internal, 'pressure group' approaches and, externally, the cultivation of a sympathetic approach on the part of the 'public'. I have earlier argued that the consensus on educational objectives which allowed the success of such efforts has been considerably undermined. If this argument is accepted, then it is plain that the NUT has to earn support for its policies by an intensive effort of popular education. In the context of the necessary trade-union campaigns to defend jobs and salaries, which, in the 'industrial' action they entail, create a risk of alienating public support, this is not an easy task. Yet any attempt to radicalise the work of the school must simultaneously attempt to create a powerful basis of support outside the school. The experience of Barking and Dagenham shows that it is possible to do this episodically, in relation to particularly stark issues. What is needed is a more systematic approach, which does not only attempt to enlist public support for the struggles of teachers, but which also tries to develop structures for a more democratic form of educational control, and which abandons teachers' claims to a near-monopoly in the definition of curricular objectives. Existing systems of control have not been without their progressive side. Statutory obligations upon LEAs, combined with a national inspectorate and regional exam boards, have prevented the grossest disparities of pre-war education re-occurring. But such systems of control have minimised popular involvement and understanding. The result is that the existing system is threatened by an unlikely but effective combination of opposites. On the one hand, there is a tendency towards greater central control of policy. On the other hand, the Conservatives are attempting to increase the weight of a 'parental choice' educated in the school of Boyson and exercised by individuals. An effective answer to these tendencies depends upon a counter-policy of democratisation. To respond, as do the Labour Party and SDP, with calls for some greater degree of parental and co-opted trade-union and 'industrial' involvement, is hardly the acme of democratic politics. To insist, as do the teaching unions, on the retention of teacher control over the curriculum, is to avoid the problems created for teachers by the new situation. More useful would be the development of policies for the democratisation of educational control. This would take a number of forms: the composition of boards of governors, in whole or in large part, through direct popular vote; direct election of members of local education committees, which would control all local educational activity, including that of the Youth Training Scheme; increased teacher and 'ancillary worker' involvement in educational planning; encouragement of school-student organisation.

Such projects, in lessening the bureaucratic aspect of educational control, do create the danger that the first fruits of educational democratisation would be harvested by reaction. Undoubtedly, there would be a tendency for radical teachers and educationally conservative communities to clash. This would be, though, a necessary and not unhealthy outcome. The recreation of a progressive popular debate about educational objectives can only proceed through the overcoming of the views that decades of isolated professionalism have allowed to accumulate both among the 'consumers' of education and among its practitioners.

To adopt such a policy would concentrate the mind of the NUT wonderfully. It would be necessary for it to make immediate efforts to appreciate popular discontent with education, and to relate its educational debates to these concerns. This would not involve a 'one-way' process, in which teachers spread enlightenment among benighted masses. Much radical criticism of education has come from particular sections of the 'community', and have implicated teachers themselves in the reproduction of unequal or oppressive schooling. The critiques of the women's movement, for instance, have forced some attempts to investigate and counteract sexual sterotyping in the school. Likewise the efforts of black parents in setting up 'supplementary schools' have exposed the failure of state education to meet the needs of ethnic minority students.[19]

Teachers and politics

The last major area of importance for transformation of the union is its relation to trade-union and political issues. Here one doubt is immediately raised: aren't most teachers, in their voting, hostile to Labour, and isn't a campaign for a more explicit political commitment – or even for a more militant type of trade unionism – a recipe for a smaller and ineffectual union? The problem is a serious one, to which there are no certain answers. A first point that could be made, though, is that from the middle 1970s onwards, the union has made a pronounced shift to the left, with many well-publicised episodes, without a disastrous loss in membership.[20] It is, in fact, in its more militant regions that the NUT has the largest share of the teaching force. There would thus seem to be no necessary connection between increasing militancy and membership loss, at any rate in the more 'advanced' areas. It is more often in the shires that membership loss is marked, though some of this could be ascribed to lack of enthusiasm for new union policies on the part of union activists in the areas.

Why, given the voting patterns of teachers, and the recruitment efforts of other unions, isn't this situation worse? One answer could lie in the difference between the political activity of voting in parliamentary elections and the activity characteristic of trade unionism. The voter enters the polling-station as an individual, whose relation to political parties is mediated through the press and television. The same person, as trade unionist, has a more active relationship to major issues, participating in branch meetings which are, at important times, very large – the average attendance at meetings of the NUT in Barking and Dagenham between 1980 and 1982 was between 150 and 200, about one-fifth of the total membership. In this situation, more depends on the relationship between union members and their 'activists' (school representatives, local elected officials) who can often successfully mediate ideas that the individual teacher would not, in the electoral arena, accept.

It could be objected that this explanation confuses politics with trade unionism. It could be argued that there is no necessary connection between trade-union militancy and political behaviour, trade unionists now being more likely to combine the militant pursuit of sectional ends with political beliefs that are by no means socialist. I do not think, however, that the objection covers the forms of trade unionism now current, if not hegemonic, in the NUT, and elsewhere in the public sector. Much of it now has a strongly political flavour: in 1980 and again in 1982, the union supported (in 1982 with considerable force) TUC days of strike action against government policies. Most issues of local and national action relate back now to quite central aspects of government policy. It is this, I think, that makes it credible to advocate the 'making political' of the union, and to argue that the defending of educational provision entails an interest in the organisation of the economy as a whole. The tendency of Mrs Thatcher's government to politicise and make controversial many aspects of social policy that were previously matters of consensus reinforces the point.

Sexual divisions

But general political campaigns aimed at government policy are not in themselves sufficient to deal with the specific divisions that occur within the membership of the NUT – in particular with the divisions between its male (mainly secondary) and its female (mainly primary) membership. Women comprise two-thirds of the union's membership. They are concentrated in the smallest and therefore often the most weakly organised schools, in the lower salary scales and 'positions of responsibility'. In the union they are under-represented. Five out of nearly fifty on the national executive are women. In activist London, out of thirty-two branch secretaries, only nine are women.[21] And while the policies of the union have paid increasing attention to 'equal opportunities', the heart of its activity – on cuts and salaries – pays little attention to women's job security or to their lower average pay. It is inconceivable that the NUT can become a truly representative force without arousing itself to a consciousness of such needs. Policies of positive discrimination in the union, and in relation to appointment and promotion (while the system of substantial pay differentials exists) are essential to such an effort. The creation of an organisation of women teachers – of a sort prefigured by the present (unofficial) 'Women in the NUT' – is an important part of any perspective that wishes to give a feminist stress to the present policies and structure of the union.

Organising – the STA

It is unsatisfactory simply to suggest the themes of a left strategy unless some attention is also paid to the agencies that can attempt to put them into practice. In the NUT, since the late 1970s and since the departure of Rank and File in what can only be described as an ultra-left direction, it has been the Socialist Teachers' Alliance (STA) which has taken most seriously the work of carrying out the tasks which the themes imply. Its initiatives – such as that on unilateral nuclear disarmament – have more and more been able to serve as the basis of alliances which bring plainly political issues into the union. Some of its members have had an important part in the creation of the 'Women in the NUT' group. Others, locally, have helped lead militant campaigns against the cuts, and in many areas form the local 'cadre' of the union.

Themes of politicisation, of feminism and of militant trade unionism have been assisted by the activity of the STA. In as much as the new left in the union now has an organising centre, it is the STA. But it would be foolish to assert that the STA is *the* left. It is more that it has been able to codify, make concrete and suggest the direction and demands of an emergent left current in the union. As the polarisation within the union develops, the STA is in a good position to present policies.

Even so, it is not possible to say that the STA has more than partially resolved the problems of a left strategy. In particular, the educational component of its work is too slender. At the time of the Great Debate the STA was quick to realise – at least in general terms – the implications of changes in state policy. It was unable, however, to move beyond commentary upon the rough pattern of change to more precise discussion of the content of its own educational policy. Just as much as the 'equal-opportunity' left, the STA's policies have in practice halted at the defence of state education against the more obvious reactionary measures. Something more is required if the traditional policies of teaching unions and of the Labour Party are to be changed.

Beyond progressive education: in the labour movement

I have outlined three types of possible development within teacher trade unionism which would allow some development of the themes discussed earlier in the book: educational content, forms of control, relationships between teachers and labour and popular organisations. Even if teachers' organisations reformed themselves, so as to combine all three themes magnificently together, it would not be enough. It is also necessary to develop some similar current of ideas in the labour movement as a whole, and, particularly, in the Labour Party. The educational policy outlined in *Labour's Programme 1982* should, despite its shortcomings, be supported in as much as its implementation would deprive the ruling class of some of its traditional privileges and strengthen the comprehensive principle in the state sector. If these policies were actively campaigned for – rather than, as in the past, entrusted for their implementation to the civil service – then that in itself, by instigating some popular involvement in the struggle for educational reform, would be a departure from the traditions of equal opportunity.

But it is necessary to go further, to question the educational content of Labour's projected reforms. Here the development of 16–19 education will be of considerable importance. It is at present both the centrepiece of the labour movement's educational perspectives and their weakest point. It is at once the means by which 'utilitarian' ideas can infiltrate and take over the education system as a whole and, potentially, the area in which a radical critique of educational purpose can be developed. Today it is helping to make the connection between school and work the major theme of English education. But, once it has been prioritised, there is no reason why this issue should be a prerogative forever of the educational right. In fact, in the context of a labour movement, part of which is now more interested in questions of economic organisation and of the labour process, its new centrality can have the effect of provoking sharper questions about education's function: why should a labour movement which speaks of sweeping changes in economic organisation and of an extension of political rights accept an education system that takes as its central feature the preparation of a workforce trained in a quite different approach to questions of production and of politics? This is a question which can quite feasibly be posed within the framework of Bennism and which would, if pursued, radicalise debate on educational policy, exerting an influence, too, upon teachers.

Beyond progressive education: in the curriculum

Finally, what, in curricular terms, should be the content of a new educational policy?

To some extent it would continue, though in a more determined fashion, to develop those aspects of state and local-authority education policy that are concerned with equalising opportunity. The Labour majority on the ILEA, according to Andy Harris, one of its members, has indicated something of what this would entail:

> We are fully aware of the curriculum areas where girls are not encouraged or expected to achieve and subsequently don't. We are aware of the power structures within our schools that show a majority of women in employment but inordinate power and responsibility is in the grip of men. We are aware of the social pyschology of mixed classroom situations where more teachers' time is given to boys. We are aware of early year conditioning in schools through the use of sexist reading books and sexist school organisation. Initial responses have been to support action/research projects that develop girls' education and anti-sexist strategies in mixed comprehensives. We have started a review of all in-service training with a view to developing anti-sexist courses and women-only promotion orientated courses. We support those schools that are getting down to producing whole school policies against sexism.[22]

While it could be objected that the strong thread of optimism running through these awarenesses is likely to snag on the awkward question of women's domestic role, it can at least be said that here are a number of immediate and practical proposals for action which can rely on fairly wide support in the school. The same can be said of the ILEA's anti-racist policy:

> The Staff Code is being looked at to enable ILEA to isolate and deal with racists in the system . . . We are increasing the number of education liaison officers . . . Their job is to work with the different black and Asian communities and to pressure ILEA for further responsive change to their needs . . . The Authority has now recognised in resource terms the right to literacy of children in both their mother tongue and second

language . . . [We will] enable further production of curriculum materials that present black kids in a positive light.[23]

Such initiatives represent the most radical 'official' curriculum development. They also suggest, especially in the area of anti-sexism, topics with which the Marxist tradition is ill at ease – a discomfort that recalls Sartre's remark that until humans reach a working age, they do not step into the realm of Marxist analysis. Beyond their more general remarks about repressive discipline, Marxists – with the notable exception of Rudolf Bahro – have had little to say about the types of human personality that the school helps to produce. By contrast, the work of feminists on the school's role in constructing or reinforcing gender stereotypes opens a way to further investigation of the means by which the school – in its selection of knowledge, in its semi-conscious prioritisation of education for boys – helps to reproduce the dominant ideologies, themselves understood in a broader and less economistic way than previously.[24] As the ILEA's efforts show, such work has suggested means by which the mechanisms of this reproduction can be identified and to some extent counteracted.

School, class and work

Concreteness of this sort is absent, however, when the question of class in education is considered. Harris continues:

> Working-class kids still come out of the system having seriously 'under-achieved'. ILEA will move on to rectifying the cultural alienation that many schools present to working-class school students and parents. I will seek to involve the manual workers' unions in detailed consideration of what the education system does to and for their children.[25]

Helpful though the last sentence is, it is doubtful whether that 'rectification' can easily be achieved, or even whether any practical thought has been given to steps – beyond the palliative – that might lessen 'alienation'. In any case, 'cultural alienation' is not a term that goes to the heart of the problem. It suggests that problem and solutions exist internally, in the official culture and the organisation of the school, rather than in the relationship between the school and the productive system, whose requirements the school serves, yet which keeps education severely at a distance from its workings. It is in this area, I would argue, that the themes of polytechnic education are of relevance, both in responding to immediate problems of 'alienation', and in laying the basis of an understanding, gained through participation, of the social relations as well as the technical processes of work. Without such an emphasis, 'cultural alienation' would be a term leading back only to the earlier progressive discussions of 'relevance'. Richard Hatcher has attempted to respond to the problem by suggesting 'changing the relationship of working class children to knowledge'.[26] He advocates a 'recomposition of the whole curriculum', so that organised activities out of school become the basis for much of the work done in classrooms:

> So, for example, a responsibility for an old or handicapped person could give rise to all sorts of study projects – on diet and budgeting, on teaching literacy or other skills, on dealing with welfare and state agencies, on the personal or social meaning of mental subnormality or old age.[27]

Such activity, he argues, would not be a merely 'practical' form of labour. It requires a combination of practical with theoretical knowledge, in which the learner operates from a position of responsibility, not dependence, in the context of a real situation, not of its imaginary or artificial school-based counterparts. His suggestions should not be assumed, therefore, to be only a more imaginative form of work experience; their function would be to help create a more general social understanding, which would not, of course, be confined to the social services – the same approach could apply to work itself.

An approach of this sort would seem to be useful in several different ways. It would lessen the immediate pressures of 'alienation'; it would allow its teacher-advocates to respond to charges that they lacked interest in all things practical or economic; it would permit a concrete discussion of the kind of education necessary for students to gain an understanding of the organisation of society in all its complexity; it would serve as the basis of a critique of the MSC's conceptions of youth training.

Significantly, though his argument derives from the polytechnic tradition, the specific example that Hatcher uses to illustrate his case – work with old people – does not relate directly to the labour process. To be of contemporary relevance, the polytechnic concept needs reformulating. It dates, in its heavy emphasis on the need to understand the productive process, from a period when the largest part of the urban workforce in Western Europe and America was engaged in the production of goods, rather than in the provision of services – and when the Soviet Union was rapidly industrialising in an effort to escape their domination. Now the balance, in the West at least, is very much the other way. In the USA in 1940, for instance, 54 per cent of employees were engaged in the production of goods. Now, only 32 per cent of the labour force are still engaged in production.[28] An education that now aspires to be polytechnic has thus to concern itself with a more complex economic organisation, and with social institutions more numerous and more pervasive in their influence than half-a-century ago.

Not only the balance between sectors of the economy has changed, but also the content of work. The rapid introduction of new technologies is transforming not only systems of production, but also systems of information, and of management. As Braverman shows, the scientific and technological content of work – mental labour – is being removed by modern methods of organisation of the workforce.[29] Understanding of aspects of production and economic organisation, either in their technical or their social connections, is thus less-than-ever possible through simple participation in workshop, office, etc. On the other hand, technological, computersised change makes it in theory more possible for the workforce and the 'consumer' to have access to stored 'mental labour' – to call upon detailed information about the productive unit or service with which they are concerned: its financing, the decisions of its management, and so on.

Yet comprehension of the organisation of work, and of the possibilities that computer technology offers for its 'mastery' by the workforce as a whole, is hardly something that enters curriculum discussion. In as much as the more advanced schools introduce general computer education, they concentrate on the one hand on its assimilation into traditional subject areas, such as mathematics, and on the other in its use as a means of updating subjects such as 'office practice'. Although this latter use certainly involves the developing of a higher level of skills than the subject has traditionally demanded, it cannot be said that schools show much concern for the computer's possibilities in assisting greater understanding of social processes. It is probable that in the same way that Crowther distinguished between the need to develop a limited number of well-qualified scientists and technicians, and the need to develop no more than a 'general mechanical intelligence' in the workforce as a whole, so contemporary education will divide the study and use of the new technology into a hierarchy of sections.

Answering the Right

I would argue, then, that the emphasis of a developing socialist policy in education should fall upon these areas. But to concentrate exclusively upon these issues would be to ignore the tactical advantage that right-wing educational ideology now enjoys in setting the terms of popular educational debate. A coherent, public, intellectual response to the Black Paper lobby is a necessary component of present socialist strategy. It should try to remove the Black Papers' claim to represent rigorous intellectual standards, and to defend, if possible, their targets.

In order to attack the Black Papers it is necessary on some points to concur with them: educational standards are too low; an education that substitutes for knowledge of nature and society a programme of socialisation and self-realisation of the entirely nugatory sort offered in many curriculum projects is incorrectly founded. The essential criticism of mass education is that it fails to convey such knowledge. The problem that has to be faced, however, is whether it can become capable of doing so, or whether, as the Black Papers, quoting T. S. Eliot, claim, the contradiction between mass education and high intellectual standards is irresolvable: 'A mass culture will always be a substitute culture; and sooner or later the deception will become apparent to the more intelligent of those upon whom this culture has been palmed off.'[30]

To refute the criticism requires, first of all, a questioning of its own credentials. The pillars of its intellectual temple are themselves shaky: a literary criticism incapable of extending itself to any systematic understanding of non-literary systems of representation, and seeing in twentieth-century culture only melancholy or ironic echoes of the past, and barbaric new forms of mass entertainment; an assimilation of history into myths of cultural decline; a bias against economic understanding, particularly in the area of present and past imperialisms. In each case, a socialist education should be able to convey a more adequate understanding. Even at present, for instance, the introduction of film and television studies into some schools has been accompanied not by a slackening of intellectual rigour but by its intensification, as teachers have attempted to create means of studying film as a medium employing systematic codes of representation. This approach, which has begun to affect the study of literature in schools, makes greater demands of the student, and without reducing cultural products to the mere reflex of social conditions, demands that texts are studied in greater historical context, with much closer attention to questions of form, and with a willingness to redefine the canons of literature. Genre, style and structure are rather more demanding terms than those of a traditional 'personally responsive' literary criticism. Likewise, in the areas of history and economics, socialists, while they can provide only the sketch of an alternative approach, can at least point to the more complex understandings demanded by a socialist response to historical and economic questions, and to the efforts already under way in some courses of 'Peace Studies', to present a complex of historical, diplomatic, technical and moral material in a way that offers some means of understanding contemporary crises.

In short, socialists take the intellectual content of mass education rather more seriously than those who pose as the defenders of standards. However, to meet Eliot's challenge, it is also necessary to show that these intellectual strengths are convertible into an educational method that could provide for Eliot's 'masses' a general, high-level culture. No kind of streaming can claim to do this for any but a minority. But the argument that non-streaming fails to offer such a culture to anyone at all must be faced. Here what is particularly at stake is 'mixed ability', or unstreamed, teaching. Claims, even if accurate, that mixed-ability teaching (MAT) minimises competition and the sense of rejection of those who fail in it would be ineffective if it was shown to lower the general level of educational achievement.

The core of a defence of MAT – a defence that still awaits its constructors – should centre on its ability to deliver an understanding to the great majority of students of the main concepts and principles of the various disciplines. It should thus compel from teachers an effort to re-present their subjects in a form that makes accessible and assimilable their founding principles. In addition, MAT should be defended as a means of resisting the stratifying effect of the division of labour upon the school. It can combat the tendency to let each 'ability' group find its 'own' appropriate level of achievement or non-achievement; even the lukewarm report of the inspectorate on MAT found that it was more conducive to the learning of 'lower-ability' students than forms of streaming.[31] This is not to say that MAT as presently constituted is an impressive achievement. We should not assume that teachers have the time, resources, belief and confidence to carry out its tasks in anything but an incomplete way. As HMI reports show, the undemanding worksheet is all too often the rule in 'mixed ability' classes – a settling for mediocrity.

Nevertheless, enough examples exist of the way in which MAT can escape from the classroom norm of the handing-down of received ideas, into a situation where the learner has an active relationship to knowledge, to give a glimpse of its possibilities. At present, MAT operates in the context of a curriculum that is still centred on the examination demands of subjects constructed on traditional lines. In the context of the kind of curriculum suggested by Hatcher's remarks, it is possible to see how it would function differently: instead of MAT having to work on the assumption that everyone should do what the academic student does, the purposes of the curriculum would be redefined so that knowledge of society and the interests and experience of the student would be brought into closer alignment.

Thus the response to Eliot's criticisms can only go so far. To claim that MAT is the means of delivering 'high culture' to the masses would be both to assume the perfections of that culture and to imply that, even in the midst of deprivation, the school can make all things possible. It remains essential to point to the cultural as well as the political and economic restrictions placed upon subordinate classes, which make advances in their cultural formation hard things to achieve. Correspondingly, it has to be argued that the achievement of such advances in a way that is at all systematic and generalised depends upon the existence of particular conditions outside the classroom. In the absence of a strong, popular current that demands a reshaped educational purpose, and of a movement among teachers that assists in developing it, it is easy for the school to tolerate the kind of 'standards' that are acceptable on the labour market, where there is no great need for a universalised excellence.

Such an argument does not exhaust the ways in which Black Paper ideas must be contested. But without attention to the question of 'standards', defence of equal opportunity and discussion of other questions of socialist educational policy are less convincing, and are open to the argument that the impossibility of the goals makes the alleged means of attaining them a wasted effort. To demonstrate successfully the validity of socialist claims in this area would have the effect of presenting a partisan approach to education in 'universal' terms, and would allow socialists to take the offensive. It would change a situation in which the left, through its continued uncritical defence of a progressive educational methodology, has been associated with the prioritising of concepts of relevance and child-centredness that have encompassed no clear intellectual objectives.

Arise . . .

I hope the reason for the book's title is now plainer. As a result of its educational ideas and its political strategy, the reforming coalition which dominated educational debate in the years 1930–70 has not been able to withstand offensives launched against it. A triple assault – of cuts, 'school-to-work' restructuring, and anti-egalitarianism – has weakened it to the point of serious debility. It seems likely, at the time of writing, that these pressures, which have since 1979 taken increasingly palpable form, will continue. Another Conservative election victory would threaten further major changes in state education, reducing and privatising provision, increasing 'choice' and selection. Even without such a victory, we could expect the continued reshaping of pre-vocational education, against a background of mass unemployment, and with an emphasis on elementary forms of post-16 education.

The starting point of any response to this situation has to be defence of the levels of provision that exist. It would be completely foolish to abstain from such an effort on the grounds that an education devoted to social control and 'grading' of the future workforce is not worth defending. It is plain that reductions in provision do nothing to improve the educational achievement of working-class children. But a defence of what exists must be combined with an attempt to change the present strategies of educational advance. Indeed, without such a change, it is difficult to see how an effective defensive movement can be built. The response to education cuts, for instance, has to depart from the pressure-group tactics of the past, to include strikes and popular mobilisation in defence of provision. The response to anti-egalitarianism must include a willingness to engage in popular discussion of educational purpose, rather than a reliance upon professional expertise. And to develop a socialist attitude to the relationship between school and work requires more than calls for expansion and modernisation – calls that have little to say about the character of education, and prepare the way only for further disillusionment in the ability of education to provide really useful knowledge.

I have found in the dominant traditions of educational reform little sensitivity to these issues. Although I am optimistic that there will be continued resistance to the grossest measures of reaction, I do not expect an easy transition 'beyond progressive education'. Yet, to look at present political and social clashes in Britain is to see not the complete rout of working-class and popular interests, but rather a process of polarisation. In the Labour Party, as in the trade unions, there are signs of a rejection of the strategies developed in periods of social consensus, and of a discussion of more radical approaches. In this context, it is possible for a new politics of education to develop. If it does, then it will help to establish and diffuse a wider sense of socialist purpose, for, as Bahro reminds us, in elaborating an educational policy, we are also setting out our aspirations for the type of society we desire.

References

Note: In the cases of pamphlets and magazine articles, page numbers are not given.

Introduction

1. A. H. Halsey, 'Expansion and Equality', in H. Silver (ed.), *Equal Opportunity in Education* (Methuen, 1973), pp. 205–8.
2. See DES, *Mixed Ability Work in Comprehensive Schools* (HMSO, 1978).
3. See The Labour Party, *Labour's Programme 1982* (Labour Party, 1982) pp. 115–33.
4. B. Simon, *The Politics of Educational Reform 1920–40* (Lawrence & Wishart, 1974).
5. H. Entwistle, *Antonio Gramsci: Conservative Schooling for Radical Politics* (Routledge & Kegan Paul, 1979).

Chapter 1: The limits of reform

1. J. Westergaard and H. Resler, *Class in a Capitalist Society* (Penguin, 1976), p. 321.
2. M. Barrett, *Women's Oppression Today* (New Left Books, 1980), p. 146.
3. *West Indian Children in Our Schools*, Interim Report of the Committee of Inquiry into the Education of Children from Ethnic Minority Groups (The Rampton Report) (HMSO, 1981), p. 52.
4. DES, *Primary Education in England* (HMSO, 1978), pp. 49, 54, 58, 73.
5. Ibid, p. vii.
6. Ibid, p. 71.
7. See *West Indian Children in Our Schools*, ch. 2.
8. Barrett, *Women's Oppression Today*, p. 141.
9. A. Gramsci, 'In Search of the Educational Principle', in *Selections from the Prison Notebooks*, ed. Q. Hoare and G. Nowell Smith (Lawrence & Wishart, 1971), p. 36.

10. P. Kellner, 'Impossible Dream of a Private School Ban', *New Statesman*, 17 April 1981.

11. A. Hopkins, *The School Debate* (Penguin, 1978), p. 23.

12. DES, *Mixed Ability Work in Comprehensive Schools*, p. 11.

13. Simon, *The Politics of Educational Reform*.

14. Ministry of Education, *15 to 18* (The Crowther Report) (HMSO, 1959), p. 449.

15. For a critique of the concept of semi-skilled labour, see H. Braverman, *Labour and Monopoly Capital* (Monthly Review Press, 1974).

16. OECD, *Educational Development Strategy in England and Wales* (OECD, 1975), p. 34.

17. DES Paper to Prime Minister, *School Education in England: Problems and Initiatives* (restricted circulation, DES, 1976), p. 10.

18. Board of Education, *The Teaching of English in England* (The Newbolt Report, 1921), quoted in M. Mathieson, *The Preachers of Culture* (Unwin, 1975), p. 74.

19. OECD, *Educational Development Strategy*, p. 34.

Chapter 2: Progressive education

1. Board of Education, *Code of Regulations for Public Elementary Schools* (1904), quoted in P. Gordon and D. Lawton, *Curriculum Change in the Nineteenth and Twentieth Centuries* (Hodder & Stoughton, 1978), p. 103.

2. *Educational Worker*, June 1927.

3. *Swansea Labour News*, 20 May 1922.

4. See G. Roderick and M. Stephens, *Education and Industry in the Nineteenth Century* (Longman, 1978).

5. *The Times Educational Supplement*, 28 February 1918, quoted in B. Simon, *Education and the Labour Movement 1870–1920* (Lawrence & Wishart, 1974), p. 344.

6. S. Macintyre, *A Proletarian Science* (Cambridge University Press, 1980), pp. 89–90.

7. H. A. L. Fisher, quoted in Simon, *Education and the Labour Movement*, p. 344.

8. Board of Education, *Secondary Education* (The Spens Report) (HMSO, 1938), p. 63.

9. See S. Bowles and H. Gintis, *Schooling in Capitalist America* (Routledge & Kegan Paul, 1976).

10. Ibid, p. 22.

11. J. Dewey, 'My Pedagogic Creed' (1897) in F. W. Garforth (ed.), *John Dewey: Selected Educational Writings* (Heinemann, 1966), pp. 44–60.

12. J. Dewey, 'The Need for an Industrial Education in an Industrial

Society' (1916) in H. L. Vassar (ed.), *A Social History of American Education*, vol. II (University of Chicago Press, 1965).

13. See Dewey, 'My Pedagogic Creed'.

14. J. Dewey, *John Dewey's Impressions of Soviet Russia and the Revolutionary World: Mexico–China–Turkey, 1929* (Columbia University Press, 1964), p. 88.

15. Ibid, p. 90.

16. Ibid.

17. W. Boyd and W. Rawson, *The Story of the New Education* (Heinemann, 1965), p. 73.

18. *The Schoolmaster*, 28 May 1926.

19. W. A. C. Stewart, *Progressives and Radicals in English Education 1750–1970* (Macmillan, 1972), p. 308.

20. Board of Education, *The Education of the Adolescent* (The Hadow Report) (HMSO, 1926), p. 107.

21. R. Selleck, *English Primary Education and the Progressives 1914–39* (Routledge & Kegan Paul, 1972), p. 26.

22. J. J. Mallon, 'Foreword' to G. A. N. Lowndes, *Margaret Macmillan* (Museum Press, 1960), p. 14.

23. Stewart, *Progressives and Radicals*, p. 23.

24. P. Nunn, *Education: Its Data and First Principles*, 3rd edn (Arnold, 1945), p. 12.

25. *Educational Worker*, January 1927.

26. Ibid.

27. Stewart, *Progressives and Radicals*, p. 432.

28. C. Freinet, 'Introduction' to 'L'école moderne française' in *Pour L'école du peuple* (Maspero, 1976).

29. Ibid, p. 6.

30. Trades Union Congress 1927, *Report of Proceedings*.

31. Selleck, *English Primary Education and the Progressives*, p. 128.

32. Lowndes, *Margaret Macmillan*, p. 116.

33. Stewart, *Progressives and Radicals*, pp. 224–6.

34. The Hadow Report, p. 88.

35. The Spens Report, p. 173.

36. P. Nunn, quoted in M. Mathieson, *The Preachers of Culture*, ch. 6.

37. F. Mulhern, *The Moment of Scrutiny* (New Left Books, 1979), p. 103.

38. Ministry of Education, *The New Secondary Education* (HMSO, 1947), p. 29.

39. Ibid.

40. DES, *Half our Future* (The Newsom Report) (HMSO, 1963), p. xvi.

41. R. Manzer, *Teachers and Politics* (Manchester University Press, 1970), p. 82.

42. B. Morris, in Schools Council, *The New Curriculum* (HMSO, 1967), p. 6.

43. Ibid.

44. Secondary Schools Examination Council, *The CSE: Some Suggestions for Teachers and Examiners* (HMSO, 1963).

45. C. James, *Young Lives at Stake* (Collins, 1968), p. 35.

46. For a discussion of the Newbolt Report (1921), see Mathieson, *The Preachers of Culture*, ch. 6.

47. The Newsom Report, p. 17.

48. Ibid, p. 6.

49. Ibid, p. xvi.

50. P. Freire, *Pedagogy of the Oppressed*; H. Kohl, *36 Children* (Penguin, 1972).

51. See F. Field, 'Britain's Urban Programme' in F. Field (ed.), *Education and the Urban Crisis* (Routledge, 1977), pp. 43–50.

52. DES, *Educational Priority*, vol. 1 (HMSO, 1972).

53. Ibid, p. 8.

54. Ibid, p. 11.

55. D. Holbrook, *English for the Rejected*, quoted in H. Kean, 'English Books', *Socialist Teacher*, 4, Spring 1977.

56. D. Barnes, *From Communication to Curriculum* (Penguin, 1976), p. 189.

57. Ibid, p. 80 – discussed in R. Hatcher, 'Language, Schools and Factories', *Radical Education*, 9, Spring 1977.

58. DES, *Educational Priority*, p. 195.

59. Westergaard and Resler, *Class in a Capitalist Society*, p. 338.

60. D. Holly, *Society, Schools and Humanity* (Paladin, 1971), p. 57.

Chapter 3: The social democratic tradition

1. R. Bahro, *The Alternative in Eastern Europe* (New Left Books, 1978), p. 285.

2. See *Labour's Programme 1982*, pp. 115–33.

3. See, for instance, Westergaard and Resler, *Class in a Capitalist Society*, and R. Miliband, *The State in Capitalist Society* (Quartet, 1973).

4. J. Seabrook, *What Went Wrong? Working People and the Ideas of the Labour Movement* (Gollancz, 1975), p. 55.

5. Gasworkers' Union pamphlet (1909), quoted in H. Kean, 'Towards a Curriculum in the Interests of the Working Class', M.A. dissertation (Institute of Education, University of London, 1981), p. 44.

6. Ibid, p. 45.

7. A. Phillips and T. Putnam, 'Education for Emancipation: The Movement for Independent Working Class Education 1900–28', *Capital and Class*, no. 10, Spring 1980, p. 27.

8. See F. Moxley, Appendix, to P. Bagwell, *The Railwaymen: A History of the NUR* (Allen & Unwin, 1963).

9. Macintyre, *A Proletarian Science*, p. 205.

10. Ibid, p. 57.

11. Independent Labour Party, *Monthly Notes for Speakers*, September 1923.

12. Labour Party Advisory Committee on Education (ACE), October 1918, quoted in Kean, 'Towards a Curriculum', p. 53.

13. R. H. Tawney, *Secondary Education for All* (Allen & Unwin, 1922), p. 64.

14. Quoted in R. Barker, *Education and Politics 1900–51: A Study of the Labour Party* (Oxford University Press, 1972), p. 149.

15. *Educational Worker*, January 1927, quoting Morgan Jones, MP.

16. See Moxley, Appendix, to Bagwell, *The Railwaymen.*

17. Trades Union Congress, *Annual Report 1927.*

18. Ibid.

19. Quoted in A. Hutt, *British Trade Unionism* (Lawrence & Wishart, 1975), p. 115.

20. Bradford Independent Labour Party, *Report of the Commission on Educational Opportunity by Bradford Labour Party* (Bradford ILP, 1929).

21. National Association of Labour Teachers, *Education: A Policy* (NALT, 1930).

22. Lord Birkenhead, 'Halifax – A Life of Lord Halifax', quoted in N. Middleton and S. Weizman, *A Place for Everyone* (Gollancz, 1976), p. 176.

23. TUC, *Education and Democracy* (TUC, 1937).

24. Simon, *The Politics of Educational Reform*, p. 372.

25. Ibid, p. 294.

26. A. J. P. Taylor, *English History 1900–45* (Penguin, 1975), p. 225.

27. British Section of the EWI, *Education at the Crossroads* (EWI, 1935).

28. G. C. T. Giles, *The New School Tie* (Pilot Press, 1946), p. 44.

29. Ibid, p. 45.

30. A. Calder, *The People's War: Britain 1939–45* (Panther, 1971), p. 627.

31. I. G. K. Fenwick, *The Comprehensive School 1944–70* (Methuen, 1976), p. 54.

32. Ibid, p. 52.

33. Giles, *The New School Tie*, p. 42.

34. Quoted in Seabrook, *What Went Wrong?*, p. 18.

35. Personal experience, Swansea 1961.

36. W. Taylor, *The Secondary Modern School* (Faber, 1963), pp. 164–9.

37. Hopkins, *The School Debate*, p. 21.

38. Fenwick, *The Comprehensive School*, p. 128.

39. *The Schoolmaster*, 17 March 1949.

40. V. Burke, *Teachers in Turmoil* (Penguin, 1971), p. 49.

41. See T. Ellis *et al.*, *William Tyndale: The Teachers' Story* (Writers & Readers, 1976).

42. For example, London Borough of Barking and Dagenham 1982; Inner London Education Authority 1978–81.

Chapter 4: The crisis in education

1. See A. Gamble, *Britain in Decline* (Macmillan, 1981), ch. 5.
2. *Education*, 20 April 1979.
3. *16–19: Learning for Life* (Labour Party, 1982), p. 3.
4. DES, *Education in Schools: A Consultative Document* (HMSO, 1977), pp. 2–4.
5. Quoted in Socialist Teachers' Alliance, *Education under the Tories* (1980).
6. DES Paper to Prime Minister 'School Education in England: Problems and Initiatives', p. 10.
7. E. Boyle and A. Crosland in conversation with M. Kogan, *The Politics of Education* (Penguin, 1971), p. 93.
8. White Paper, *A Framework for Expansion* (HMSO, 1972), p. 1.
9. OECD, *Educational Development Strategy in England and Wales*, p. 43.
10. Ibid, p. 38.
11. James Callaghan, speech at Ruskin College, Oxford, October 1976, quoted in STA, *Education under the Tories*.
12. The first Black Paper was *The Fight for Education*, ed. C. B. Cox and A. E. Dyson (Critical Quarterly Society, 1969).
13. See B. Coard, *How the West Indian Child is made Educationally Sub-normal in the British School System* (New Beacon Books, 1971).
14. Hopkins, *The School Debate*, ch. 1.
15. See N. Wright, *Progress in Education* (Croom Helm, 1977).
16. K. Amis, 'Why Lucky Jim Turned Right', in *What Became of Jane Austen, and Other Questions* (Penguin, 1981), p. 198.
17. K. Amis, 'Postscript' to 'Lone Voices' in *What Became of Jane Austen* (p. 167) explains that the 'maxim' was in fact a misquotation of his original 'More will mean worse'.
18. For instance, D. Walker in *Black Paper 1977*, ed. C. B. Cox and R. Boyson (Temple Smith, 1977), pp. 38–41.
19. Amis, 'Why Lucky Jim Turned Right', p. 198.
20. See, for example, D. Rubinstein (ed.), *Education and Equality* (Penguin, 1979).
21. See Ellis *et al.*, *William Tyndale: The Teachers' Story*; and J. Gretton and M. Jackson, *William Tyndale: Collapse of a School or a System?* (Allen & Unwin, 1976).
22. Hopkins, *The School Debate*, ch. 1.
23. Ibid, p. 25.
24. Ibid, p. 27.
25. Ibid, p. 26.
26. See STA, *Education under the Tories*.
27. *Education*, 27 April 1979.
28. N. St-J. Stevas, *Better Schools for All* (Conservative Party, 1977).
29. Ibid.
30. *Education*, 27 April 1979.
31. D. Walker, *Black Paper 1977*, p. 41.

32. *Education*, 27 April 1979.

33. See C. Chitty, '16–19: Learning for Life', *Forum for the Discussion of New Trends in Education*, vol. 25, no. 1, Autumn 1982.

34. J. Fairley, 'The Decline of Industrial Training', *Forum*, vol. 25, no. 1, Autumn 1982.

35. Quoted in ibid.

36. See Appendix to Manpower Services Commission, *Youth Task Group Report* (MSC, 1982).

37. Fairley, 'The Decline of Industrial Training'.

38. N. Kinnock, speech to Socialist Educational Association fringe meeting at Labour Party Conference 1979.

39. Labour Party, *16–19: Learning for Life*, p. 4.

40. DES, *Progress in Education* (HMSO, 1978), p. 15.

41. TUC, *Note of Comment on the Government's Consultative Paper 'Education in Schools'* (TUC, 1977).

42. *The Teacher*, 19 October 1979.

43. NUT, 'Education: The Great Debate' (duplicated paper, 1977).

44. NUT Memorandum, 'Priorities and Decision-Taking in the DES', Tenth Report of Expenditure Committee of the House of Commons, Session 1975–6, *Policy-making in the DES* (HMSO, 1976), pp. 129–41.

45. NUT, 'Education: The Great Debate'.

46. D. Lawton, *The Politics of the School Curriculum* (Routledge & Kegan Paul, 1980); Wright, *Progress in Education*; B. Simon, articles in *Marxism Today*, June 1976, February 1977, July 1977, February 1980.

47. *Rank and File Teacher*, no. 50, February 1977.

Chapter 5: Socialist alternatives

1. Leah Manning, MP, quoted in *Educational Worker*, January 1927.

2. Nan McMillan, unpublished memoir of David Capper.

3. See the compilation, *L'internationale communiste et l'école de classe*, ed. D. Lindenberg (Maspero, 1972).

4. Quoted in S. Nearing, *Education in Soviet Russia* (Plebs League, 1926).

5. Ibid, p. 96.

6. Ibid, pp. 97–8.

7. Ibid, p. 118.

8. Quoted in S. Castles and W. Wustenberg, *The Education of the Future* (Pluto Press, 1979), pp. 62–3.

9. Ibid, p. 50.

10. See A. Phillips and T. Putnam 'Education for Emancipation', *Capital and Class*, 10, Spring 1980, pp. 18–42.

11. A. N. Pierotti, *The Story of the NUWT* (NUWT, 1963).

12. Ibid.

13. See Selleck, *English Primary Education and the Progressives*.

14. *Educational Worker*, November 1926.

15. *Educational Worker*, June 1927.

16. *Educational Worker*, March 1928.

17. Lindenberg, *L'internationale communiste et l'école de classe*, p. 57.

18. Ibid, p. 61.

19. *Educational Worker*, May 1928.

20. Ibid.

21. *The Schoolmasters' Review*, September 1919.

22. *Educational Worker*, December 1927.

23. *The Schoolmaster*, 21 May 1926.

24. Ibid.

25. S. Macintyre, *Little Moscows: Communism and Working Class Militancy in Inter-War Britain* (Croom Helm, 1980), p. 164.

26. A. Tropp, *The School Teachers* (Heinemann, 1957), p. 227.

27. Manzer, *Teachers and Politics*, p. 46; J. Hinton and R. Hyman, *Trade Unions and Revolution* (Pluto Press, 1975), p. 39.

28. See Simon, *The Politics of Educational Reform*, chs 1 and 2.

29. Quoted in L. Trotsky, *The Struggle against Fascism in Germany* (Pathfinder Press, 1971), p. 158.

30. *Educational Worker*, October 1929.

31. *Educational Worker*, June 1930.

32. Ibid.

33. F. Claudin, *The Communist Movement from Comintern to Cominform* (Penguin, 1975), p. 195.

34. British Section of the EWI, *Schools at the Crossroads*.

35. Ibid.

36. Giles, *The New School Tie*, p. 111.

37. Fenwick, *The Comprehensive School*, p. 52.

38. CPGB, *Education: Communist Party Policy* (CPGB, 1959).

39. M. Morris, *Your Children's Future* (Lawrence & Wishart, 1953), p. 10.

40. *The Schoolmaster*, 14 October 1948, 4 November 1948, 17 March 1949.

41. W. Roy, *The Teachers' Union* (Schoolmaster Publishing Co., 1968), p. 115.

42. Fenwick, *The Comprehensive School*, pp. 115–17.

43. Roy, *The Teachers' Union*, p. 142.

44. M. David, *The State, the Family and Education* (Routledge & Kegan Paul, 1980), pp. 164–5.

45. 'What We Stand For', in *Rank and File Teacher*, no. 21, Autumn 1972.

46. Ibid.

47. See *Rank and File Teacher*, no. 2, June 1968.

48. Ibid.

49. T. Cliff, 'You Can't Have a Rank and File Movement if the Factories are Empty', *Socialist Review*, May–June 1982.

50. Rank and File Teacher, *Teachers' Salaries, the Fight for a Single Scale* (Rank and File, 1974).

51. Ibid.

52. *Rank and File Teacher*, no. 33, September 1974.

53. Cliff, 'You Can't Have a Rank and File Movement', estimates a print run of 3,000, implying a circulation of about 2,000.

54. 'Statutes of the EWI' (1922) in Lindenberg, *L'internationale communiste et l'école de classe*, p. 59.

55. *Educational Worker*, December 1926.

56. See M. Starr, *Lies and Hate in Education* (London: Hogarth Press, 1929).

57. *Educational Worker*, January 1927.

58. *Educational Worker*, November 1927.

59. *Educational Worker*, July–August 1929.

60. *Educational Worker*, May 1928.

61. *Educational Worker*, October 1928.

62. Lindenberg, *L'internationale communiste et l'école de classe*, p. 57.

63. *Educational Worker*, October 1929.

64. *Educational Worker*, June 1930.

65. *Rank and File Teacher*, no. 5, April 1969.

66. *Rank and File Teacher*, no. 21, August 1972.

67. *Rank and File Teacher*, no. 40, June–July 1975.

68. Ibid.

69. Teachers Against the Nazis, *Tankits* (London, 1978).

70. *Rank and File Teacher*, no. 21, Autumn 1972.

71. *Teaching London Kids*, no. 14.

72. Keith Kimberley, talk at North-East London Polytechnic, July 1980.

73. See, for instance, *Teaching London Kids*, nos 9, 12, 13, 14.

74. Editorial, *Teaching London Kids*, no. 9.

75. E. P. Thompson, 'Peculiarities of the English', in *The Poverty of Theory and Other Essays* (Merlin Press, 1978), p. 71.

76. A. Gramsci, 'Syndicalism and the Councils', in *Selections from Political Writings 1910–20*, ed. Q. Hoare (Lawrence & Wishart 1977), p. 110.

77. See Holbrook, *English for the Rejected*, cited in Kean, 'English Books', *Socialist Teacher*, 4, Spring 1977.

Chapter 6: Beyond progressive education

1. Bahro, *The Alternative in Eastern Europe*, p. 284.

2. *The Times Educational Supplement*, 10 September 1982.

3. *The Times Educational Supplement*, 2 July 1982.

4. MSC, *Youth Task Group Report*.

5. DES, *17+: A New Qualification* (HMSO, 1982).

6. MSC, *Youth Task Group Report*.

7. Ibid.

8. DES, *17+: A New Qualification*.

9. MSC, *Youth Task Group Report*.

10. Education Group, Centre for Contemporary Cultural Studies, *Unpopular Education: Schooling and Social Democracy since 1944* (Hutchinson, 1981), pp. 255–6.

11. NUT, *Annual Report for 1982* (NUT, 1982), p. 216.

12. Ibid, pp. 216–17.

13. *The Teacher*, 30 April 1982.

14. *The Times Educational Supplement*, 31 July 1981.

15. *The Times Educational Supplement*, 4 June 1982.

16. *Educational Worker*, June 1929.

17. See *Socialist Teacher*, no. 11, Summer 1980, for discussion of press coverage of this event.

18. *The Times Educational Supplement*, 11 June 1982.

19. See Coard, *How the West Indian Child*.

20. *The Times Educational Supplement*, 24 September 1982, makes an assessment of the numerical strength of the teachers' unions.

21. NUT, *Annual Report for 1982*, pp. 369–74.

22. *London Labour Briefing*, no. 23, October 1982.

23. Ibid.

24. See, for instance, D. Spender, *Invisible Women* (Writers & Readers, 1982).

25. *London Labour Briefing*, no. 23, October 1982.

26. R. Hatcher, 'What Kind of Schooling for Youth?', *Socialist Teacher*, no. 13, Spring 1981.

27. Ibid.

28. E. Ginzberg, 'The Mechanisation of Work', *Scientific American*, vol. 247, no. 3, September 1982.

29. Braverman, *Labour and Monopoly Capital*.

30. T. S. Eliot, quoted in *Black Paper 3*, ed. Cox and Boyson, p. 96.

31. DES, *Mixed Ability Work in Comprehensive Schools*.

Index